Istanbul 2011

© Erkam Publications 2009 / 1429 H
Published by:

Erkam Publications
Ikitelli Organize Sanayi Bölgesi
Turgut Özal Cd. No: 117/4
Ikitelli, Istanbul, Turkey
Tel: (90-212) 671-0700 pbx
Fax: (90-212) 671-0717
E-mail: english@altinoluk.com
Web site: http://www.altinoluk.com

ISBN: 978-9944-83-138-3

The author   : Osman Nûri Topbaş
Translator   : Songül Özlem Şahin
Copy Editor   : Adurrahman Candan
Graphics   : Rasim Shakirov (Worldgraphics)
Printed by   : Erkam Printhouse

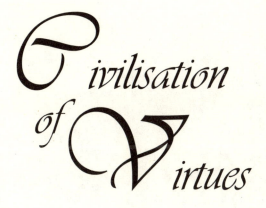

Civilisation of Virtues

- I -

Osman Nûri TOPBAŞ

CONTENTS

PROLOGUE

Eternal thanks and praise be to Allah Most High for making the worth of all creatures, and in particular that of mankind, reach its peak with the Blessed Prophet, and Who, in swearing by the life of that Eternal Pride of the Universe, made Him a source of dignity and honor and who gave us the good fortune to be from his community.

Eternal peace and blessings be upon the Sultan of Prophets, Muhammad Mustafa, the mercy of all the worlds and the source of blessings, the one who crowned good character, displaying innumerable examples of virtuous behaviour and who was given an everlasting and unique model character for all of mankind.

Everything to be found in the heavens and the earth has been prepared especially for mankind. As such he should consequently live in a state worthy of and grateful for this divine favour. The way to do this is by serving Him as a virtuous and noble servant. The essence of this servanthood is '*makarim-i akhlak*' a character praised and adorned with the best of behavior…

The Prophet Muhammad ﷺ (saw)[1] has said:

"*I was sent for no other reason than to complete good character*". (Muwatta, Good Character, 8)

Thus he expressed the fundamental wisdom in his duty and he stressed the importance of good character. It is indeed so, that

---

1.   *SAW* in Arabic is short for "*sallallahu alayhi wa sallam*" and means "peace and blessings be upon him". It is pronounced whenever the name of the Prophet is mentioned. (translator's note).

from whichever aspect we look, the entire life of the Prophet ﷺ is like an exhibition of ultimate ideals, traits and merits.

Almighty Allah confirmed this truth by stating:

"O My Messenger. Indeed you are truly vast in character". (Qalam, 68:4)

Consequently the Prophet was not just a teacher teaching the Qur'an in word only. Rather he practiced what he preached and was thus a living Qur'an and a guide, who taught the divine truths through his actions. This is why his dignified and blessed life is the best of examples for future generations to come until the Day of Judgement.

With the appearance of the Prophet, that Light of Creation, the dark horizons of the world were enveloped in light, a new morning of bliss awaited by mankind was born, hearts were enlightened, reflection became deeper, and discernment broadened. In short, it was he ﷺ who allowed the human being to attain to his true nobility and dignity, and to goodness and merit, to the truth, to justice and to virtue. It was he ﷺ who taught the secret of life and eternity.

Because no other prophet would come until the Day of Judgment, whatever beauty and virtue it is that mankind is in need of, have all been bestowed upon His superior person. From this point of view then, all goodness has reached its peak in him. Consequently:

He is the peak of love. He is the peak of courage. He is the peak of patience and perseverance. He is the peak of generosity, sacrifice, and putting others first. He is the peak of abstinence, scrupulousness, contentedness and humility even though great booty and worldly bounties were laid out before him. He is the peak of mercy and compassion and helping the needy. He is the peak of sincerity and piety. He is the peak of gaining Allah's pleasure and he is the peak of gratitude. He is the peak of knowledge of Allah and wisdom, and grace and favour. He is the peak of prophet hood. He is the peak of teaching and education of divine etiquette and good manners. He is the peak of being the physician of wounded hearts. He is the peak of righteousness and trust. He is the peak of being the friend of Allah and His beloved. He is the leader of all people on the Day of Judgement. He is the intercessor of the offenders. He is the peak of all manner of virtues, character and service. In other words, only He can be at the peak of the most perfect servanthood.

Every characteristic, behavior and virtue that constitutes good character of which Allah is well pleased, has been revealed to mankind through the blessed tongue and application of the Prophet.

Almighty Allah displayed the model of the 'perfect human' in the person of the Prophet ﷺ. This was what He intended with Islam and so He made him a model person for all of mankind.

In this way the words and principles of the Prophet constitute a collection of the most perfect examples lived in his own life and also lived by action in the lives of his community which will continue on until the end of time.

In contrast to this, those philosophers whose minds have not been trained by revelation, and their ideas, – both positive and negative - about social peace and tranquility and character have been left in the books on the dusty shelves of libraries. And the lives of those who have applied them have been rather short. At any rate, these philosophers have not been able to practice what they have preached, neither have they been able to show examples from other people's lives. Their ideas have remained mere theories.

For instance Aristotle laid down the foundations for certain rules and regulations of moral philosophy, but these were removed from divine revelation. Consequently we do not see even one person who has applied this philosophy to his own life, having attained to happiness. Even the most important book of Farabi, which includes his hypothetical ideas on a city of virtues and the ideal republic have never had the chance to be applied and those ideas have not been able to emerge out of the lines of the book. Because these truths were not written down and spoken from experience, neither have they been applicable after being written down.

Whereas the Prophet ﷺ had endeared himself to everyone even before his duty of prophethood had begun and his personality was of such perfection that it caused the people to say "You are the trustworthy and loyal one". Thus he began his duty of preaching after this open confirmation of his identity and character.

And thus it was through his elevated character and spiritual training that centuries and generations were reshaped; and humanity was presented with an 'era of bliss'. One of the most important names in Islamic legal methodology, Karafi (v. 684), has the following to say:

"If the Messenger of Allah ﷺ had no other miracle, the generation of noble companions that he reared would have been enough to prove that he was a prophet".

The essence of the Prophet, his words and his every state, from beginning to end, are a personified account of the beautiful character that is hidden in the Holy Qur'an. The most perfect and ultimate examples of all virtues were displayed in his life.

The greatest artwork of almighty Allah is mankind himself. And the peak of spiritual perfection of mankind is the Blessed Prophet ﷺ. This is the case to such a degree that Almighty Allah accepts, and proclaims as such, that obedience to the Prophet is on a par with obedience to His own Being and rebellion against the Prophet is equal to rebellion against Allah Himself.

It is stated in the Holy Qur'an:

'Say, "If you love Allah, then follow me and Allah will love you and forgive you for your wrong actions. Allah is Ever-Forgiving, Most Merciful' (Al'i Imran, 3:31)

Accordingly, all praise of the Blessed Prophet is permissible as long as one does not go so far as to commit *shirk*, or associating partners with Allah. Nevertheless our praise of him will reflect on our tongues only to the degree that we truly comprehend him.

At the head of the list of those who were able to comprehend in the best possible way – and within the limits of human ability - the Messenger of Allah, are his Blessed Companions. It is they who have transmitted traces of him to us. It was these blessed people who had the duty of transmitting to subsequent generations the beauty in the worship, social relations, and dealings of the Messenger of Allah ﷺ. They had the honour of conversing with him. The Blessed Prophet spoke of them as being 'like the stars in the heavens'.

Because they received a share of the prophetic character of the Messenger of Allah ﷺ, his Companions understood that the true wealth one possesses was relative to how much of good deeds one sent to the afterlife. Thus they were able to display unrivalled virtues such as generosity, thinking of others, and sacrifice for the sake of gaining the pleasure of Allah. They concentrated their lives on gaining Allah's pleasure and, by acting with compassion and mercy, they reached the peak of justice.

The most pleasurable and meaningful moments in the lives of that blessed generation were the moments when they were able to spread, with great enthusiasm in their faith, the message of the unity of Allah to mankind.

After the generation of Companions, all of the *awliyaullah* (friends of Allah) that will continue on until the end of time, have followed beautifully their principles of virtue. Thus they have and will be exalted due to the blessings that come from prospering in the Sun of Virtue that is the Messenger of Allah.

How beautifully Jalaladdin Rumi expressed this state:

"Come o heart! The true celebration is the union with the Blessed Muhammad. For the enlightenment of the world has come from the light of the beauty of that blessed person".

The scholars and Gnostics who are the friends of Allah, and who have attained to the honour of being the heirs of the prophets, are paramount in terms of prophetic guidance and perfect behaviour manifested throughout the ages. That is, they too are virtuous guides, real and embodied for the rest of mankind who have not had the honour of seeing the Blessed Prophet and his Companions.

In short, it is without a doubt that the prophets exemplify the virtues that give life to hearts. As their leader we find the Prophet Muhammad (pbuh) at the altar. In the next lot of rows and chains of virtue are those sincere scholars, righteous slaves, gnostics, and lovers etc, according to the degree of their attachment to him. They are the elite personalities due to their servanthood and beautiful lives of goodness. Because they too have lived beautifully with sincerity, they have presented to those around them rare memories of beauty that will never depart. In this way they have formed a 'civilisation of virtues'. The stories of virtue that are transmitted from them give peace of mind to the spirit and bestow healing upon ailing hearts.

Consequently Abu Hanifa has the following to say about mentioning stories about virtue, a method that the Qur'an uses.

"*Stories that tell of the beauties of the righteous scholars are more pleasing to me than most of jurisprudence. Because these stories teach us the etiquette and character of those who have become close to Allah*".

It is true that it is impossible for a person to truly comprehend a matter without being given an example. Good and evil are only made clear in the light of examples. Love becomes more lively and exuberant. Imbibing oneself in the character of one's beloved can only be realized through the beautiful example that they project. In this respect good examples are divine favours that allow one to reach true nobility and dignity.

Along the same vein, Malik bin Dinar ﷺ has the following to say:

"*The beautiful stories of righteous slaves are like gifts from heaven*".

Consequently each story of virtue is like a priceless pearl that has been presented to us as a gift.

In short, it is most important that we build good character and virtues. To this end the Prophet ﷺ has the following to say:

"*On the Day of Judgement there will weigh nothing heavier in the scales of the believer than good character. Allah Most High is displeased with the one who commits ugly acts and who speaks ugly words*". (Tirmidhi, Birr, 62/2002)

The essence of good character emerges, undoubtedly by befriending the Blessed Prophet and those righteous slaves who walked in his footsteps. This is the first condition in holding on to the chain of virtues. What constitutes the essence of ugly character is to lose their friendship and to destroy oneself in the current of ignorance. On the basis of this truth, Almighty Allah has the following to say in a *hadith qudsi*[2] :

"*I have waged war against the one who is hostile to those whom I have befriended (who serve Me in all sincerity). My servant draws nearer to Me with nothing more pleasing to Me than what I have made obligatory upon him, and then continues to draw nearer to Me with supererogatory devotions until I love him; and when I love him I become his hearing with which he hears, his sight with which he sees, his hand with which he strikes, and his foot with which he walks, so that by Me he hears, by Me he sees, by Me he strikes, and by Me he walks. Should he ask Me I should surely grant him his request; should he ask Me for protection I shall surely protect him. Never do I hesitate[3] in anything as I hesitate in taking the soul of my believing servant; he dislikes death and I dislike to displease him...* (See Bukhari, Rikak, 38; Ahmad, VI, 256; Haysami, II, 248).

In order for us to attain to the superior virtues that will make us acceptable to Allah, we must nourish heartfelt love for the friends of Allah and the Blessed Prophet ﷺ to whom they are devoted. And it is him that we must follow.

For this reason it is hoped that, as we become truly acquainted with the Prophet ﷺ and take as our model his superior characteristics, which have been praised by Allah, we will have the honour of being amongst those 'brothers' that the Prophet gave glad tidings of.

If we recognize him today, he ﷺ will recognize us tomorrow in that great gathering on the last Day. If we reach a state in which

---

2. A *hadith qudsi* is a *hadith* whose words are from the Prophet but whose meaning has been either revealed or inspired to him (Translators note)

3. Almighty Allah is certainly above human characteristics such as hesitation. This expression has been used here to show the attention and care that He shows the slaves that He loves and to allow comprehension for human perception.

we see him in reality then he will see us. If we listen to him and do as he says, then he will hear our cries and take us by the hand. In this way we will become for others, an exhibition of his beautiful example. This is the greatest virtue of all!

❁

This book was written as a modest attempt to show these examples of virtue in this framework. The examples given consist primarily of the sublime examples from the exalted personality of the Prophet Muhammad ﷺ and then His Companions, the saints, the scholars and the righteous who are like smooth mirrors, reflecting his beautiful example.

In addition, we have not been restricted to the examples solely from the Prophet nor from those friends of Allah who have walked in the path of piety. We have also attempted to occasionally cite examples from historical figures, shaped and formed by political and social events and heroes who have had a role to play in the direction of the world. This is in order that those who find themselves involved in such situations can find models of ideal behavior they may be in need of.

To properly convey that Sultan of both worlds ﷺ in whom all of the chains of virtue gather and from whose elevated personality a share has been distributed to other masters of virtue is obviously very difficult for us incapable ones. In any case, we know that we are incapable of portraying him completely. Rather our aim is to taste a droplet of that ocean of enlightenment, to move a few more steps closer to Him, to recharge our ardor and love for Him, to express our devotion to Him, to run to His endless Mercy, and to seek refuge in His intercession…

We thank almighty Allah that he has honoured us helpless and feeble servants with being from amongst the community of the Beloved Prophet ﷺ. Having grasped the truth of this divine favour, the only way to be worthy of the Messenger of Allah's love and to fulfill the compliment of being from amongst his 'brothers' is to embrace his practices and, like his heirs, the saints, to adopt his prophetic character to the best of our ability.

This is why we need today to imbue ourselves with love for the Messenger of Allah and be seekers in training for his exalted character just like the Companions and friends of Allah. We must strive to live and make live their beauty which will never fade nor grow old, no matter how many centuries pass. This is the price to pay in order to be worthy of the fortune and honour of being one of the true community of the Pride of the Universe.

I would like to thank all of my academic brothers, particularly Murat Kaya, who have had a role to play in the preparation of this work. I pray that their efforts will be accepted as ongoing charity by Allah.

May Almighty Allah bestow on us a life illuminated by beautiful behavior and samples of virtue which will be a source of gaining His good pleasure. May He render us a close friend in every respect of His Messenger in both worlds. And may he allow us to attain to his great intercession....

Amen...

Osman Nuri Topbas
May 2006
Uskudar

Part 1

Faith and Worship

1. To Live one's faith with a passion

Faith is the light of the intellect, the polish of the consciousness and the harmony of the emotions in the heart. Passing happily from this temporary world to the eternal realm will be possible only under the guidance of faith.

The guides of faith are the Prophets, the divine books and the friends of Allah who have ordered their lives according to the first two. It is only through the fervour of faith that the prophets, the saints and the righteous throughout history have been able to become living examples of the manifestation of achievable virtues.

Faith is a divine favour; trials in this life are a standard by which to measure the degree of soundness of one's faith. The preservation of one's faith with the patience and submission which are to be expected from a believer is the price to pay for the attainment of divine rewards. That is, Allah Most High desires that a price be paid by his servants in order for them to perceive the loftiness and value of the bounty of faith that he has bestowed upon them.

'Allah has bought from the believers their selves [lives] and their wealth in return for the Garden'. (Tawba, 9:111).

This verse is an evident expression of this truth.

Consequently the means to perfecting one's faith is the willing sacrifice in His path of the price desired by Allah (one's life, property, belongings etc) in order to gain His pleasure.

Overcoming all of the difficulties and struggles that the trials of life have to offer with contentedness and submission and following in the path of Allah and His Messenger is the most important sign of the believers.

Each believer is obliged to pay a price to Allah Most High for the bounty of faith. To assume ownership or to expect recompense for something which one has not paid the price for is to pass one's time in triviality.

The rise towards the peak of faith is dependent on performing good deeds, living with good intention, worship and beautiful behaviour that aims to please Allah. This is why in the Holy Qur'an and in the *ahadith*[4], faith and good deeds have generally been mentioned together. Faith can be lived not with dry facts and theory but rather with truths that are felt and perceived, embroidered onto the heart and then reflected in one's behavior. Pondering and reflecting on the flow of divine power throughout the universe results in a heart that is suitable for worship and renders the believers able to taste true faith and become subject to endless manifestations of virtue throughout their lives.

Faith is the greatest of all forms of worship because worship is possible only through faith. Worship is carried out at specific times. The prayer too, the most virtuous of all deeds, is obligatory five times a day. Faith, however, is required constantly and thus it is necessary to keep it alive in our hearts at every instant. This is why we must avoid the trap of all manner of sins that lead the heart into heedlessness, and keep our faith protected by good deeds (which are like spiritual armour).

The jewel of faith is the most precious of assets for the believer. Satan, who in the Qur'an is proclaimed to be our open enemy,

---

4. *Ahadith* is the plural form of *hadith* which are the collection of sayings of the Prophet Muhammad ﷺ (Translators note)

together with his accomplices, tries at every opportunity to steal that jewel of faith from the hearts of the believers with various tricks and whisperings. From this perspective then, it is a most crucial duty to be constantly vigilant of our hearts and embrace our faith with great love and zeal. We must strive to protect it and render it unshakeable with good deeds.

In order for our jewel of faith to reflect the manifestations of Allah like a pure and bright mirror we need 'zikrullah' (remembrance of Allah). *Zikrullah* is like embroidering the word '*Allah*' on our hearts with love and yearning. In this way, the rust of sins and heedlessness will be erased from the heart and it will taste the true pleasure of faith due to it having attained to complete peace and contentedness.

The joy that arises out of the faith of those blessed and special servants who have attained to such a spiritual maturity is above all other fleeting pleasures and enjoyment. Moreover, all of the burning pain and suffering of this world is virtually non-existent in their eyes.

Let us now peruse some of the innumerable examples of patience, forbearance, fortitude, insight, sacrifice and aspiration displayed by the Messenger of Allah ﷺ who taught us our faith, and those righteous believers whose service has made it possible for this bounty to reach our day:

Scenes of virtue

When the Messenger of Allah ﷺ was a child of a mere 12 years, Bahira the Monk said to him:

"Dear child, I am asking you in the name of Lat and Uzza[5] to answer me".

---

5. Lat and Uzza were two of the main idols in Mecca. (Translators note)

He replied: "Do not ask me anything in the name of Lat and Uzza. By Allah! I abhor nothing as much as I abhor those two idols".

Even at such a young age the Prophet distanced himself from idols and unbelief with the sound nature that he carried within him. The exceptional resolution and effort that he showed in living his faith with a passion, and spreading and teaching it, after becoming a prophet is a fact every believer is aware of.

❁

The sorcerers at the time of the Pharaoh rejected his claim to divinity and as a result were subject to unbearable torture. However they were able to challenge him due to the courage that came from their faith:

"Your oppression is in this world only. You are free to judge and do as you wish. In any case we will be returned to our Lord".

At the command of the Pharaoh their hands and legs were cut off diagonally. Before they were hung onto the branches of palm trees, they raised their hands to the heavens in a display of human weakness. Anxious that they **would be weak in faith they prayed:**

"...O our Sustainer! Shower us with patience in adversity, and make us die as men who have surrendered themselves unto Thee". (A'raf 7:126)

Thus they sought refuge in Almighty Allah and were reunited with their Lord in the boundless pleasure to be found in martyrdom.

❁

The first Christians who were sincere Muslims preserved their faith amongst the jaws of circus lions and they too tasted martyrdom with a passion.

❁

Another group at the head of the list of heroes who lived their faith with a passion, were believers who were burned alive by the 'People of Ukhdud'. The Jew, Dhu Nawas, who was the King of Yemen in the 4th century AD, forced the people of Najran, Christians devoted to the faith of monotheism (the Oneness of Allah), to change their beliefs. When they resisted, many of them were burned alive, having been thrown into pits of fire. It is reported that the number of people who died in this way reached 20 thousand.

These oppressors were named the 'People of the Pits' after the pits (called 'ukhdud') that they dug in order to burn the believers. But those who tried to destroy the faith that had become unyielding and which was engraved upon the hearts, failed and instead became subject to the vengeance and punishment of Allah. They were thus overcome and ruined, damned for eternity. Almighty Allah states:

'**They destroy (but) themselves, they who would ready a pit of fire fiercely burning (for all who have attained to faith**' (al-Buruj, 85:4-5)

❁

Sumayya ﷺ, a female Companion, who lived her faith with a passion in the Era of Bliss, was fortunate in attaining to the title of 'the first female martyr of Islam'. Sumayya ﷺ (ra)[6] used to be very afraid of the mere prick of a needle. However, after she had tasted the sublime pleasure to be found in faith, she displayed great tolerance in the face of the red hot rods of iron that the polytheists[7]

---

6. *ra* short for *radiyallahu anhu* (for males) and *anha* (for females). It means 'may Allah be pleased with him or her' and is used as a term of respect for the Companions of the Prophet Muhammad (translator's note).

7. In arabic '*mushrik*', a person who commits the greatest sin, namely that of '*shirk*', which means to associate partners with Allah. Many of the Quraysh, the tribe of the Prophet Muhammad were polytheists (Translator's note).

branded her with, not once compromising her faith. After being subjected to such savage torture, one of her legs was tied to a camel, and the other leg tied to another and she was torn apart brutishly, thus becoming a martyr in a terribly painful way. Her husband, Yasir, also showed unbearable patience even though he was very old and weak. He too eventually tasted martyrdom. In fact the family of Yasir (may Allah be pleased with them) became the first martyrs of Islam. They paid the price of their faith by living it with a passion.

❁

Even as the blood poured forth from the body of Bilal ﷺ, which had become like jelly from the heavy torture of the wild and angry *polytheists*, he continued in his call to monotheism: "*Ahad, Ahad, Ahad*: Allah is one, Allah is one, Allah is one". Beyond the pain and torture, he was experiencing the pleasure of meeting Allah, having tasted the sublime delight of faith.

❁

During his caliphate Omar ﷺ asked one of the first Muslims, Habbab bin Arat ﷺ:

"Can you tell us a little of the torture that you experienced in the way of Allah".

Habbab replied:

"O Commander of the Believers! Take a look at my back".

Having looked at his back Omar was horrified. He said:

"Never in my life have I seen a human back so disfigured".

Habbab continued:

"The unbelievers would light a fire and then put me into it with no clothes on. The fire was eventually extinguished when the melted fat from my body dripped onto it".

The polytheists would put rocks that they had heated in fire onto Habbab's back and the skin of this blessed Companion would peel off due to the intensity of this torture. Despite this he still refused to speak the words desired by the unbelievers. This is because the excitement of wuslat (meeting with Allah) that is vouchsafed by faith wipes away all worldly suffering.

Habbab bin Arat narrates:

One day when the Messenger of Allah ﷺ was in the shade of the Ka'bah, we went to him and complained to him about the torture we had suffered at the hands of the polytheists. After that we asked him to ask for Allah's help in saving us from this torture. He ﷺ said in reply:

"Amongst the generations before you were believers who were burned and thrown into pits, and then sawed into two from head to toe and whose flesh was raked with iron combs but who yet did not turn back from their faith. I swear by Allah, that He will complete this religion and make it reign supreme to such a degree that a person will be able to travel in safety from San'a to Hadramat fearing nothing but Allah and the attack of his sheep by wolves. But yet you are impatient..." (Bukhari, Manakibu'l Ansar 29, Manakib 25, Ikrah 1; Abu Dawud, Jihad 97/2649)

❋

The enemies of Islam would beat Suhayb ﷺ until he fainted. This torture continued until the migration to Madina. Eventually Suhayb was able to embark on his journey in the aim of emigrating to Madina after the Prophet. Some of the Meccans followed him and reaching him they said:

"You came here as a poor and weak person. You attained to great wealth amongst us. And now you want to go and take your wealth with you? By Allah we will never allow it!

Suhayb immediately got down from his animal. Taking out some arrows from his quiver he said to them:

"O people of Quraysh! You know that I am the best archer amongst you. And by Allah I will use up all of the arrows I have with me and when they are finished I will draw my sword. Whilst I am in possession of both of these none of you will be able to come close to me. Only after they have left me can you do as you wish to me. Now, if I tell you where I have left my treasure will you let me go?

The polytheists accepted his offer. After that Suhayb told them where his treasure was and continued on his journey. It was the middle of the month of Rabiul awwal when he reached Quba (a village near Madina), and was reunited with the Messenger of Allah ﷺ.

When the Messenger of Allah ﷺ saw him he smiled and, implying that he had sacrificed all of his wealth in the cause of his faith he said:

"Suhayb has triumphed! Suhayb has triumphed! O Father of Yahya. Your trade has proven profitable. Your trade has proven profitable".

According to the narrations, the following verse was revealed after this event:

'But there is (also) a kind of man who would willingly sell his own self in order to please Allah; and Allah is most compassionate towards His servants' (Baqara, 2: 207)

Zinnura Hatun ؓ was another female companion who suffered a thousand torments and cruelty at the hands of the polytheists. She was left blind due to the torture carried out by Abu Jahl.

Abu Jahl said to her:

"Do you see? Lat and Uzza have blinded you".

Zinnura Hatun replied:

"No! By Allah! They are not the ones who have made me blind. Neither Lat nor Uzza can benefit or harm me. My Lord is capable of restoring my eyesight!"

When the morning came the polytheists, whose souls were enveloped in eternal darkness, were amazed to see Zinnura Hatun's eyesight restored by the grace of Allah.

Many more of the first Muslims suffered such pain and torment. Such eminent Companions of the Prophet such as Amir bin Fuhayra, Abu Fukayha, Mikdad bin Amr, Ummu Ubeys, Lubeyna Hatun, Nahdiye Hatun and her daughter, were subject to extreme unimaginable torture. The polytheists would tie their feet with chains and drag them out naked, laying them down in the desert at the time of the most intense heat, and placing large rocks upon them. They would implement all forms of torture until they lost consciousness and did not know what they were saying. They would strangle them and not stop until they believed them to be dead.

These blessed Companions managed to preserve their faith in the face of unbearable torture and oppression. They struggled with their property and their lives so that this divine favour could reach us. This is because they were in a state of true perception of the greatness of the bounty of Islam. Thus they knew how to open the door of divine dignity in both worlds. Their mortal lives came to an end and they entered into eternal happiness having embodied the following divine command:

'O you who have attained to faith! Be conscious of Allah with all the consciousness that is due to Him and do not allow death to overtake you ere you have surrendered yourselves unto Him' (Al'i Imran, 3:102)

❋

Sa'd bin Abi Waqqas ﷺ was a son who was completely obedient towards his mother. On entering Islam his mother said to him:

"O Sa'd! What have you done? If you do not renounce this new religion, I swear I will neither eat nor drink and eventually die. And because of me, you will be known as the son who killed his mother.

Sa'd ﷺ replied: "Mother please, I will not leave this religion for anything". Hearing this, his mother did not eat for two days and two nights and lost a lot of strength. In order to make his mother, whom he loved very much, give up her obstinacy, Sa'd said to her with firm resolution:

"Dearest mother! Know this: Even if you had 100 lives and you lost them all one by one, I would never abandon this religion…"

On seeing the resolution of her son, his mother gave up her obstinacy and started to eat once more. After this event, the following verses were revealed:

'And (Allah says): We have enjoined upon man goodness towards his parents: his mother bore him by bearing strain upon strain and his utter dependence on her lasted two years: (hence O man), be grateful towards Me and towards thy parents, (and remember that) with Me is all journeys' end. (Revere thy parents) yet should they endeavour to make thee ascribe divinity, side by side with Me, to something which their mind cannot accept (as divine), obey them not; but (even then) bear them company in this world's life with kindness, and follow the path of those who turn towards Me. In the end, unto Me you all must return; and thereupon I shall make you (truly) understand all that you were doing (in life)' (Loqman, 31:14-15)

✼

At the time when the Prophet was about to emigrate to Madina he called Ali and told him of the divine command to emigrate. After that he informed him that he was leaving him as his trustee so that he could return all of the property that was left in trust to him. This was because there hardly remained a person in Mecca who, having something valuable, did not entrust it to the Messenger of Allah, knowing his truth and honesty.

As a precaution against the plans of the polytheists, the Messenger of Allah ﷺ said to Ali:

"O Ali! Sleep in my bed tonight. And cover yourself with this cloak of mine. Fear not! Nothing you dislike will happen to you".

With great courage of faith, Ali ﷺ slept in the Prophet's bed under the shadow of the fierce spears that were ready to rain down on his body. The fiercely angry polytheists who had come to the Prophet's house were determined to murder the Messenger of Allah. On seeing Ali under the covers they became enraged:

"O Ali! Where is your uncle's son"? they shouted.

Ali ﷺ said:

"I know not. I have not an idea. And I am not a watcher over him. You told him to leave Mecca. And so he did".

Upon this they berated and harassed Ali; in fact they took him to the Masjid al Haram and imprisoned him for a while before they let him go.

✼

On one occasion the people of Najd came to the Prophet ﷺ and informing him of their desire to learn Islam, requested a teacher. Upon this, Allah's Messenger sent them about 70 *hafiz*[8] who were from the *Ahl as-Suffah*[9]. They all knew Islam extremely well. When the Muslims came to Bi'r-i Mauna in order to take a rest in a cave they were ambushed. A spear thrown by a polytheist called Jabbar bin Sulma, entered the back of Amir bin Fuheyra and came out through his breast. On realizing that he was about to become a martyr, Ibn-i Fuheyra, a mere 40 years old at the time, shouted out in extreme delight:

"By Allah, I have triumphed!"

Ibn-i Tufayl, who was the chief of those who had prepared this treacherous trap, took one of the Muslims who had escaped the massacre, and brought him to one of the martyrs, asking him:

"Who is this?"

The Muslim replied:

"It is Amir bin Fuheyra".

"I saw his body being raised to the sky. I can still see him hovering there between the heavens and the earth. Then he was laid back down".

Despite being witness to such an event, Ibn Tufayl, a famous poet, failed to become Muslim. However Jabbar, who had made a martyr out of Amir bin Fuheyra, eventually became a Muslim. The shouts of the person he had made a martyr of, "I have triumphed" rang in his ears for days. These words became an enigma for him. "I just killed him and he is saying that he has tri-

---

8.   A hafiz is a Muslim who has memorised the entire Qur'an (Translator's note)

9.   Literally "the people of the bench". The ahl as-Suffa were a group of early Muslims who had nowhere to live and no means of sustenance. Thus they used to live on a bench outside the Prophet's mosque (Translator's note).

umphed. How can this be so?" he thought to himself for weeks on end. One day he asked Dahhak bin Sufyan, famous for his bravery and fellow citizen of the Prophet who thought him worthy of 100 hundred people. What did this Companion mean when he said: "By Allah I have triumphed"? When he replied that it meant "I have reached Paradise", Jabbar woke up from the deep sleep of heedlessness he had been in and became Muslim.

At the end of the Battle of Uhud, Safiyya 鸞 wished to see her brother Hamza 鸞 whose body was in pieces. With this intention in mind, she turned towards where the martyrs were located. Her son, Zubayr met her and said:

"The Messenger of Allah commands you to turn back".

"Why? So that I do not see my brother? I know in what terrible way he was torn apart and dismembered. He was afflicted with this misfortune for the sake of Allah. And anyway, nothing other than this can give us consolation. Allah willing I will bear it and await the reward from Allah" she said.

Zubayr went to the Messenger and informed him of what his mother had said. The Prophet said:

"In that case let her go see her brother".

Safiyya then went to the corpse of her brother, honoured with being the master of martyrs, and prayed wholeheartedly for him.

The courageous faith of the blessed Companions who took the letters written by the Messenger of Allah 鸞 to various rulers of the time has become very famous. They delivered the Prophet's message, having fear of no one but Allah in the face of oppressors who were famous throughout the world and executioners ready to cut off heads. They did not refrain from speaking bravely in the shadow of spears and lances. Some examples are as follows:

One day the Messenger of Allah ﷺ asked:

"O people. Who will take this letter to the Muqawqis of Alexandria in anticipation of Allah's reward and recompense?

Hatib bin Abi Beltaa ﷺ scrambled up and approached the presence of the Prophet:

"O Messenger of Allah! I will take it" he said

Allah's Messenger said:

"O Hatib! May Allah bless you in this duty".

When Hatib bin Abi Beltaa arrived in Alexandria he read the Prophet's letter to the King. Muqawqis called Hatib to his side and also gathered together his men of religion. Let us listen to the rest of the story from the words of Hatib:

"The Muqawqis said to me:

"I am going to speak to you about some things that I wish to understand".

"Please let us talk" I said to him

The Muqawqis asked:

"Isn't your master a prophet?"

"Yes. He is the Messenger of Allah" I replied.

"If he is truly a prophet then why did not he pray to Allah against his people who forced him to seek refuge in another land having exiled him from his own land?"

I replied:

"You would bear witness that Jesus, the son of Mary was a prophet, correct? If he was truly a prophet then should he not have prayed to Allah to destroy his people who caught him and wanted to crucify him, instead of being raised to the heavens?"

The Muqawqis could find no answer. After he was silent in thought for a while he asked me to repeat my words. After I repeated what I had said the Muqawqis thought again for a period. After that he said:

"You have spoken well. You are a sage, you speak appropriately and you have come from one who must also be a sage".

Following that I said to the Muqawqis:

"Before you there was a man who claimed that he was the most supreme god. Allah Most High caught that Pharaoh and punished him in both this world and the next. You should take heed from those before you and not be a lesson for those who come after you".

The Muqawqis said:

"We have our religion and we cannot leave it until we see something better than it".

To this I said:

"Islam is most certainly above the religion that you practise. We invite you to Islam, the religion that Allah Most High chose for his people. Muhammad Mustafa ﷺ invites not only you, but all of mankind. The people that were the harshest and crudest to him were the people of Quraysh. And the people that were the most hostile to him were the Jews. However those who are the closest to him are the Christians. Just as Moses heralded Jesus, so too Jesus gave good news of the coming of Muhammad ﷺ. Our calling you to the Qur'an is like you calling to the Gospels those who follow the Torah. Everybody should follow the prophet who was sent in his own time. You too are one who is living at the time of Muhammed 🕮. Consequently by calling you to Islam we do not want to separate you from the religion of Jesus. On the contrary, we are proposing that you do what is appropriate to the message that he brought".

The Muqawqis said:

"I have studied the religion of this prophet. I have seen that he neither commands to withdraw from the world nor does he forbid what is liked and accepted. He is neither a sorcerer who has lost his way, nor is he a liar who claims to have knowledge of the unseen. On the contrary there are signs that he is a prophet, as he has uncovered news from the unseen. However I still wish to reflect for a little while longer" he said.

Later he wrote a reply to the letter of the Prophet...However, the Muqawqis did not do more than this, neither did he become Muslim. And to me he issued this warning:

"Be careful! Do not let the Coptics hear a single word from you, lest they cause you harm".

What a beautiful example are these words of Hatib. What an example of the foresight and bravery of a believer who lived his faith with a passion and who spoke with the courage of faith in front of a King.

✼

The letter written to the Chosroes of Iran was taken by Abdullah bin Huzafa 🕮. On seeing the name of the Prophet being written before his own name, the Chosroes got angry and tore that blessed letter into pieces. He also insulted the envoy with harsh words.

With the courage and dignity that came from his faith, Abdullah addressed Chosroes and his men as follows:

"O people of Persia! You are passing your numbered days without prophet or book. You control a mere portion of the land that is in your hands. You are living life as a dream. Whereas the portion of earth that you are not in control of, is much greater.

"O Chosroes! Many a ruler came before you who reigned and desired either this world or the hereafter. Those who wanted the hereafter received their share in this world as well. Those who desired this world lost their hereafter too. You belittle this religion that we are proposing for you but by Allah wherever you may be, when that thing which you belittle befalls you, you will be terrified and you will not be able to protect yourself.

In response Chosroes said that property and kingdom were particular to him only and that he wasn't afraid of being defeated nor that anyone would claim partnership with him. Following that he ordered his men to throw Abdullah bin Huzafe outside.

As soon as he had left the presence of Chosroes, Abdullah mounted his horse and headed for Madina, with the following thoughts passing through his mind:

"By Allah I am not worried about either outcome for me (whether to be killed or to remain alive). I have carried out my duty of delivering the Messenger of Allah's letter and that is all that matters".

This is the peaceful state of the conscience of one of the heroes of Islam who risked his life in order to fulfill a wish of Allah's Messenger.

❁

Here is another story full of lessons to be taken, and displaying the peerless virtue and the courage of faith of Abdullah bin Huzafe:

During the caliphate of Omar, a Muslim army was sent against the Romans in the Qaysariyye district of Damascus. Abdullah bin Huzafe was in that army. The Romans had taken him hostage. They took him to their king and said:

"This is a companion of Muhammed".

After having Abdullah locked up in confinement with no food or drink, he then sent to him a portion of wine and some pork. They watched him for three days. Abdullah neither placed a hand on the wine nor the pork. They said to the King:

"He has lost much strength now. If you do not take him out of there, he will die".

The King had him brought to him and asked him:

"What prevented you from eating and drinking?

Abdullah answered:

"Actually necessity had made the eating of those things lawful for me, yet I did not want to make neither myself nor Islam a laughing stock in front of you".

In response to this dignified attitude, the King said:

"What if you become a Christian and I give you half of my wealth, and if I make you a partner in all my kingdom and then I give my daughter to you in marriage?"

Abdullah replied:

"Even if you give me all of your wealth and in fact all of the wealth of Arabia, I would never turn away from the religion of Muhammad ﷺ for the blinking of an eye".

The King said:

"In that case I will have you killed".

To which Abdullah replied:

"That is for you to decide".

Abdullah was then hung up on a crucifix. First of all the archers flung arrows at him but purposefully missed him in order to scare him. Then he was offered the chance to become Christian once more. That blessed Companion did not show even the slightest of tendencies. Upon this the King said:

"Either you become Christian or I will place you in a cauldron of boiling water".

When he refused again, a boiling cauldron made of copper was brought forth. The King had one of the Muslim slaves brought to him. He offered that he become Christian. When the slave rejected this offer he was thrown into the cauldron. Abdullah was watching. His skin instantly peeled away from his bones and came off.

The King again suggested to Abdullah that he become Christian. When he refused once more, he ordered that he be thrown into the cauldron. Just as Abdullah was about to be thrown into the cauldron, he began to cry. Thinking that he had changed his mind, the King had Abdullah brought to him and offered that he become Christian once more. When he saw how violently Abdullah refused, he asked in shock:

"Then why did you cry"?

Abdullah gave this superb reply:

"Do not think that I cried out of fear of what you wished to do to me. No. I cried because I only have one life to give in the path of Allah. I said to myself: "You have only one life and it is about to be thrown into that cauldron. In just an instant you are going to die in Allah's cause. Whereas how I wish I had had lives to the number of hairs on my body, so that all of these lives could be sacrificed in order to gain Allah's pleasure".

This awesome act displayed by Abdullah due to his courage of faith and dignity impressed the King and he wished to let him go free.

"Kiss my head so that I may let you go", he said

To this offer that could have no objection, Abdullah replied with an offer of his own:

"Will you let all of the other Muslim slaves go free together with me?"

When the King replied that he would, Abdullah said:

"In that case I will".

Abdullah says later:

"I said to myself: "What objection could there be to my kissing the head of one of Allah's enemies in order to free my own life and the lives of the Muslim slaves? Kiss it and be free".

That day 80 Muslim slaves were set free. When they returned to Omar they told him what had happened. Omar said:

"To kiss the head of Abdullah bin Huzafe is a duty incumbent upon every Muslim! I will be the first to carry out this duty". He thus got up and went to Abdullah and kissed his head.

Muslims who possess insight and discernment, observe events through the window of the afterlife. They can do this because their faith offers them a broad perspective. In this way they constantly take account of the positives and negatives, that is the benefit and harm. This is why all the worldly pain and suffering, and fleeting ordeals and distress are not worthy of mention against their love of faith.

Another hero who lived his faith with passion is Wahb bin Kabshah ﷺ. The tomb of this blessed companion is in China. The Prophet sent him to China with the duty of propagating Islam. But at that time it used to take one year to reach China from Madina. After reaching China and staying there for a long time spreading Islam, he set out on the road back to Madina in order to satisfy, albeit slightly, the longing he had to see the Messenger of Allah. After an arduous journey that took one year he arrived in Madina. But alas he was unable to see the blessed Prophet as he had passed away. He returned to China, his longing having increased even more. This he did in order to complete the sacred duty he was commanded to do by Allah's Messenger. He passed away while carrying out this duty. In this way, Wahb bin Kabshah was honoured with being the first representative of Allah's Messenger in China. His mortal body remained in China however his eternal spirit went to the enlightened Madina to be together with the spirit of the Messenger of Allah ﷺ.

The events that took place between Sultan Bayazid II and his brother Jem Sultan openly reflect the courage of faith of our fore-fathers and the beauty and virtue that Islam bestowed upon them:

Becoming a sultan in the year 1481, Bayazid II (who was even known as Bayazid the Saint due to his piety) spent the first 14 years of his sultanate dealing with the problems that arose as a result of his brother Jem Sultan's claims to the Ottoman throne. This situation hindered Bayazid II from active participation in the Christian world. Jem Sultan proposed the following to Bayazid II:

"Let us divide our country into two. You rule over half and I will rule over the other half".

Bayazid II replied, rejecting his offer:

"My brother, this country is the property of the people. If we divide it, the government will lose power. We will become a series of weak principalities. This will have grave consequences. I would divide my body but the land of my people cannot be divided".

A short time after that Jem Sultan was invited to Rhodes by the Knights of Rhodes. He was impressed by their polite words and heedlessly accepted their invitation. However the Knights broke the promises they had made and sold him to the Papacy like a slave. The Papacy were planning to use the prince in the next crusade against the Ottomans. However, realising that he was not going to be successful in this, Pope Innocent suggested that Jem Sultan become Christian. This offer greatly offended Jem Sultan. Deeply saddened he said to the Pope:

"Even if you give me the whole world, and not just the Ottoman Sultanate, I would never change my religion".

The supplication that Jem Sultan made to Almighty Allah when he realised that the Crusaders wanted to use him against Islam is sufficient to show the aspiration of his efforts for his religion:

"O my Sustainer! If it is the case that the unbelievers wish to use me as a tool to bring harm to the Muslim world, then do not let this slave of yours live any longer. Take my soul to your honourable abode as soon as possible..."

His prayers must have been answered for at the age of 36 he passed away in Naples. In his last days, his last testament he made to those near him was as follows:

"Make sure to announce the news of my death all over the land. Do this for certain so that the games that the unbelievers wish to play with the Muslims, using me as a tool, can be over. After that, go to my brother Sultan Bayazid. Request that, however difficult it may be, he transports my body back to our country.

I do not wish to be buried in the land of the unbelievers. Whatever has happened until now has happened. Make sure that he does not refuse this request of mine. Ask him to pay all of my debts. I do not want to go the Divine Presence in debt. Let him forgive my family, my children and those who served me. Let him make them content according to their states".

His brother Bayazid II carried out his final testament.

These are the qualities that Islam bestows upon the human being. The reciprocal relationship between these two brothers displays their devotion to their faith and their love of their country. It is also a demonstration of sacrifice for the sake of the peace of their people, and an example of tolerance, the accounting of the conscience that results after realising one's mistake, refraining from violating another's rights, forgiveness and compassion amongst many other virtues.

❋

The brothers Ilyas, Oruc and Hizir had an important place in the Ottoman navy. They were busy with sea trade before they opened up the banner of jihad in the Mediterranean. However, this business presented a great danger for the Mediterranean. When Oruc Reis was enslaved by Rhodesian pirates, his brother Hizir Reis began to search for a solution. Despite having sent large ransoms for his brother's freedom, due to the tricks of the deceitful pirates who did not keep their word, his brother's enslavement took a long time. Not content with this, the unbelievers sent to Oruc Reis a priest who had the audacity to suggest that he become Christian. However the reply of Oruc Reis was like a slap across their faces:

"O ignorant fools! How could I leave a true religion in order to become a member of a false one?

The pirates became angry at this and said:

"In that case let your Muhammad come and save you" and chaining him to a skiff they made him a gallery slave.

Seeking refuge in Allah, Oruc Reis prayed:

"Just wait and see how my Sustainer will help me".

A little while later with the help of a group of individuals wearing white kaftans and green turbans also visible to the unbelievers, his hands and feet were unchained and he was left free in the deep ocean and freed from slavery. In this way he attained to the bounty of the submission and reliance that comes from the strength of faith. After this event Oruc Reis, together with his brother Hizir Reis began a merciless battle against the pirates of the Mediterranean.

The Battle of the Dardanels is another superb example which illustrates the manifestations of living one's faith with a passion.

A retired colonel who was a commander in the Dardanels battle and who was wounded in the process, explains in his memoirs as follows:

"It was one of the days in which the Battle of the Dardanels was being fought. That day the battle, which lasted until the evening, was to result in our victory, despite the disproportionate superiority of the enemy in material terms. I was following excitedly the last stage of the battle from my observing point. The cries of "Allah, Allah" of the Muslim soldiers vibrated on the horizon and these awesome shouts were even able to drown out the sound of the cannon balls that represented the entire grandeur of a frightening civilisation.

At one point I heard the sound of footsteps next to me. When I looked back I came face to face with Sergeant Ali. There was terrible pain written all over his pale, yellow face. Before I had the chance to

ask him what was wrong, he showed me his arm which was enough to explain everything. I shivered with terror. His left arm was about to fall off four finger lengths from his wrist from where he was hit. It was only a thin piece of skin that stopped his hand from falling to the floor. Sergeant Ali was grinding his teeth, trying to overcome the pain. He handed me the pocket-knife he carried in his right hand:

"Cut it off Commander!" he said

This statement of just three words expressed such a terrible wish and such necessity that I grabbed the knife almost unwillingly, without even thinking and separated the hand that was hanging by its skin from his arm. While carrying out this blood curdling task I tried to lift his morale:

"Do not be distressed Sergeant Ali. May Allah restore health to your body".

Not long after that, Sergeant Ali sacrificed not only his hand for his people but also his blessed body. As he closed his eyes, repeating the following sentences, he was surrounded by a pool of blood as he took his last breath:

"May my Muslim nation live long! May Allah keep it from straying from faith... May my life be sacrificed for my religion!"

And so it was that with faith in their breast the Ottoman soldiers in the Dardanels, viewed the defence of their nation as a debt and requirement of their religion and did not refrain from paying this debt with their lives. This is why these soldiers embraced their religion as they did their guns, and they embraced their guns as they did their faith.

During the Battle for the Dardanelles, the Roman Mecidiye Bastion was almost completely wiped out as a result of a terrifying assault by the enemy. Much of their arsenal had been blown up into the air and sixteen artillery men were martyred. Only the captain and two soldiers remained of the entire battalion along with a cannon whose crane had been broken and which was not able to take in any cannonballs.

The captain had gone to inform the surrounding troops of their situation. Koca Sayyid, one of the soldiers, looked out at the enemy ships that were advancing over the sea spewing out fire and death and sighed deeply. His eyes filled with tears. His sorrowful heart quivered with the pain of helplessness in not being able to do anything in the face of the enemy and he raised his hands up to Allah and prayed:

"O my Sustainer! O Allah who is the Possessor of Might! Give me such strength at this moment that none of your servants be as strong as I".

Suddenly it was as if Koca Sayyid had departed from this world... It was as if he were in the presence of his Lord and none other. The tears fell from his eyes over his cheeks. For a while he chanted: "*There is no power nor might except by Allah*".

Then, all of a sudden he shouted "*Allah!*" and to the surprise and amazed look of his friend he reached for the 215 *okka* (approximately 276kg) canon ball and lifted it up. He climbed and then descended the iron steps three times. The crackling of his breast and shoulder bones could be heard. Pouring out sweat on the one hand, he was praying to Allah with cracked lips:

"O Allah! Please don't take away my strength".

Eventually the fate of that battle changed with the 3rd famous cannon ball that he placed in the mouth of the cannon. The Ocean, the name of the English armoured battle ship, had been hit and had been enveloped in fiery flames.

Learning of this event Cevat Pasha praised Almighty Allah, then congratulated Koca Sayyid and requested that he lift another cannon ball of the same weight. Koca Sayyid gave the following reply:

"My Pasha! When I lifted that cannon ball my heart was filled with the success of Allah and my body was subjected to divine help. I was a different person. Almighty Allah's help and providence became manifest in response to the supplication I made to Him. This was an event particular to that moment. I cannot lift it now, Captain; you must excuse me please..."

At these words of Sayyid, Cevat Pasha said:

"My son! You have performed a very successful task. Ask me for some reward".

This devoted hero who had erased all but servanthood to Allah from his heart, displayed even more heroism with the following words:

"My Captain! I have no request; however due to my build which is like a wrestler, one loaf of bread a day is not enough for me. Could you give orders that they give me two loaves so that I can be stronger against the enemy?"

Cevat Pasha, smiling at this request, granted him his wish. When evening fell and everyone received one loaf of bread and Colonel Sayyid received two, the heart of this great hero of faith could not accept this. In times of scarcity of food he did not want to be different from his friends. He returned one of the loaves given to him and never again took two loaves.

What a pure and brilliant heart!...Undoubtedly this state of Koca Sayyid was an embodied expression of his sincerity and devotedness that came from the courage of his faith.

✳

To sum up, faith is not merely a dry declaration. Faith is a witness to the degree and perfection of a believer's heart. And its sign is self-sacrifice and devotion. Because faith is eternal capital, many lives have been sacrificed and unbearable torture and difficulties undergone throughout history in order to preserve and strengthen it. Unparalleled examples of virtue and heroism have been displayed for the sake of Allah. And today what we need more than anything else is this excitement of living faith with passion and fervour. As a debt of gratitude for the bounty of faith that has been bestowed upon us, we need to mobilise ourselves in order to invite all of humanity to *Dar-us Salaam* or the Abode of Peace. A believer who lives his faith with passion will feel responsible for the state of the community. Allah willing, we will attain to the divine reunion in the hereafter to the degree of our sacrifice for the perfection of our faith in this fleeting world.

May Almighty Allah make us all of those who attain to the perfection of our faith and make us servants who spend their lives to this end... Amen!

2. Sincerity[10]

The Messenger of Allah ﷺ said: *"Actions are according to their intentions"* (Bukhari, Faith, 41; Muslim, Imare, 155)

As a result the essence of all good deeds, and primarily worship is that they are carried out in order to seek the pleasure of Allah. This can only take place with sincerity. In other words, it is only through sincerity and connection to a lofty aim that it is possible to raise the status of one's deeds to the level of worship. Consequently the real condition for the acceptance of one's deeds in the eyes of Allah is sincerity.

---

10. In Arabic *ikhlas*, from the root word (*khalasa*) which means to be pure, unmixed, and unadulterated. (translator's note)

Sincerity is the performance of deeds for the sole purpose of pleasing Allah and abstaining from spoiling them with carnal desires and worldly aims. The spirit is to the body what sincerity is to deeds. An insincere deed amounts to nothing more than tiring oneself in vain, and becomes devoid of essence.

Sincerity is to preserve the heart from all manner of worldly benefit with the aim of moving closer to Almighty Allah. Sincerity is to purify one's deeds from all manner of spiritual blemishes, namely ostentation (*riya*) and pride (*ujub*), because these are diseases of the heart that destroy and contaminate one's sincerity.

To erase from the heart all aspirations other than seeking the pleasure of almighty Allah is an essential duty incumbent upon every Muslim. However, one must be careful about the following, which is that those in possession of sincerity are in constant danger of losing this beautiful state as a result of the triumph of the *nafs*[11]. Just as it is extremely difficult to remain at the top, so too it is hard to preserve one's sincerity. The words of Zunnun Misri in regards to this matter are famous:

'All people are dead, except for the scholars (those who know). All scholars are asleep, except for those who act on their knowledge. All those who act on their knowledge are at risk of being deceived, except those who have sincerity. And those who have sincerity are in perpetual danger in this world...'[12]

However those servants who are able to maintain their sincerity in spite of all manner of difficulty, are subject to much divine favours.

In short, sincerity allows one to attain to the greatest good, namely divine pleasure. Because Allah's aim for people's deeds is

---

11. The nafs is the soul of the human being that inclines towards evil. It is the carnal and animal nature of the human being (translator's note).

12. Bayhaki, ShuAbu'l- Iman, Beirut 1990 V 345

that they carry them out for the sole purpose of gaining His pleasure. It is stated in the Holy Qur'an:

'We have sent down the Book to you with truth. So worship Allah, making your religion sincerely His' (Az- Zumar, 39:2)

'Say: "I am commanded to worship Allah, making my religion sincerely His' (Az-Zumar, 39:11)

Sincerity saves a believer from the assault of Satan, his greatest enemy, because Satan can only plague the one who is weak in his sincerity. Allah says in the Holy Qur'an:

'He (Satan) said, "My Lord, because You misled me, I will make things on the earth seem good to them and I will mislead them all, every one of them, except Your slaves among them who are sincere.' (Al-Hijr, 15: 39-40)

Those who possess sincerity will be saved from the fire of hell.

Almighty Allah gives glad tidings of this truth in the following verse:

'You will definitely taste the painful punishment...except for Allah's sincere servants' (As-Saffat, 37: 39-40)

However small it may be, a deed done with sincerity, is enough to save the one who performs it. The Messenger of Allah ﷺ has stated:

"Be sincere in your religion! If you do this, even small deeds will be enough for you". (Hakim, IV, 341)

Sincerity attracts divine help. The Prophet ﷺ has also stated:

"Allah helps this community due to the supplication, ritual prayers and sincerity of the weak". (Nesa'i, 43)

One should not doubt that sincerity will bring triumph. This is because sincere efforts will always be preserved and are never in vain. Throughout history there have been many small armies consisting of sincere and forbearing individuals that have triumphed, with the permission of Allah, over other armies much greater in number and better equipped. This situation shows that sincerity is the foundation of victory.

Scenes of Virtue

The life of the Messenger of Allah ﷺ is filled with examples of the peak of sincerity. The following event that took place in the first days of his duty expresses this beautifully:

The polytheists wanted to send news to the Prophet ﷺ through his uncle, Abu Talib, in order to make him abandon his task of preaching. The Prophet ﷺ gave the following reply to his uncle:

"O my uncle! By Allah, even if they put the sun in my right hand and the moon in my left in order to make me abandon the religion of Allah, I would never abandon this course of mine! Either Almighty Allah will spread it throughout the world and my duty will be ended or I will die in this path".

The polytheists, uneasy at this birth of Islam, and having their attempts through Abu Talib meet with failure, then went to the Messenger of Allah ﷺ directly with the audacity to offer the following:

"If it is riches you want, we shall give you all the wealth you desire; such that there will be no one amongst the tribes richer than you.

"If you are after leadership we shall make you our leader; and you shall be the ruler of Mecca.

"If you desire to marry honourable women, we will give you whichever of the beautiful women of Quraysh that you desire.

"We are willing to do whatever you want so long as you abandon this course".

The Messenger of Allah ﷺ, in answer to all the lowly and sensual suggestions that those heedless people made and would further make, stated the following:

"I desire nothing from you. I want neither wealth, nor property, nor kingdom, nor leadership, nor any woman! The only thing I desire is for you to abandon your worship of pathetic idols and worship Allah alone".

The Prophet ﷺ lived his life struggling to spread the religion of Allah and for this reason he remained independent of people and never desired anything for his own person. Prophet Muhammad ﷺ and the other prophets all repeated the following words:

"I do not ask you for any wage for it. My wage is the responsibility of none other than the Lord of all the worlds"[13].

The following scene from the life of Prophet Moses is another magnificent display of sincerity:

Almighty Allah said:

"When he arrived at the water of Madyan, he found a crowd of people drawing water there. Standing apart from them, he found two women, holding back their sheep. He said, "What are you two doing here?" They said, "We cannot draw water until the shepherds have driven off their sheep. You see, our father is a very old man". (Kassas, 28: 23)

These two women were Safura and Sufayra, the daughters of Prophet Shuayb ﷺ. Despite going hungry for eight days, Moses

---

13. (As-Shu'ara verses 109, 127, 145, 164, 180. Jonah verse 72, Hud verse 29)

(عَلَيْهِ السَّلاَم) drew water from the well enduring great hardship, and watered their animals. The women thanked him and left.

Later Shuayb invited Moses to his house for a meal. Moses was hesitant about eating though he had been hungry for days. Shuayb asked the reason. Moses answered:

"We are such a family that if we were to be given the entire world we would never exchange it for one deed of the hereafter. I did not help you in anticipation of this meal but rather to seek the pleasure of Allah".

Shuayb was very pleased with this answer and said:

"This offer of ours is not because you helped us but because you are our guest. Come let us eat".

At this, the tired and hungry Moses accepted the offer to eat.

This example demonstrates the necessity of refraining from tainting the sincerity in one's intentions with any worldly expectations in order not to lose the reward of good deeds done for the sake of Allah.

❋

Wasila bin Aska ﷺ tells of an example of sincerity that took place during the campaign for Tabuk:

When it was the time to head out for Tabuk, I had neither material wealth nor an animal to mount. I did not wish to be deprived of this blessed campaign so I cried out in Madina:

"Who will let me ride their mount in return for my share of the booty?"

An old man from the Ansar said that he would let me take turns riding his animal and thereby take me to the battle. When I immediately said: "We have a deal" he responded:

"In that case come and walk with me, by the blessings of Allah".

Thus I had made a good friend and so I set out with him. As a result Allah favoured me with booty: some camels fell to my lot. I led these to that old man from the Ansar. He said to me:

"Take your camels with you!"

"But according to the deal we made at the start, these are yours" I told him. Alas however much I repeated these words, the Ansari replied:

"O my brother! Take your booty, it was not this that I desired. My intention was to share in the reward from Allah, that is, I wanted to be a partner in your spiritual gain". (Abu Dawud, 113/2676)

Those blessed Companions, who generously donated all that they had in order to please Allah, complied with their utmost to the secret of sincerity, whether it was whilst setting out for battle in the name of Allah or helping a believing brother.

They showed the greatest care in ensuring that the slightest shadow of any fleeting worldly benefit should not fall over the good deeds that they did for Allah.

✻

Whenever Aisha ❊ helped the poor she would respond to the prayers for goodness made by the poor with a prayer of her own. She was asked about this:

"You give to them and you also pray for them. What is the reason for this?"

She responded:

"I fear that the prayer that they make will be the recompense for the charity I give. I make the same prayer that they make so that I can anticipate my reward only from Allah".

What an excellent example of sincerity!...Those blessed people showed the utmost care in preserving their sincerity.

❖

How superb is the following display of depth and sensitivity of the sincerity of Ali ﷺ:

During a battle Ali had captured an enemy soldier and was about to kill him. The man suddenly spat on the blessed and radiant face of Ali, in response to the nasty inclination that had arisen within him.

It would have been mere child's play for that brave and gallant 'lion of Allah' to cut off the head of that enemy with one fell swoop. However Ali stopped suddenly, anxious that at that moment his *nafs* had tainted his intention which was to fight for Allah and nothing else. He stopped and slowly put down his sword, which had been named Zulfikar and had been a gift to him from the Prophet, deciding not to kill his enemy.

The shocked man on the ground lay in a wretched state awaiting his death. He had thought that Ali would display an even more intense effort with greater anger and rage as a result of his spitting in his face. However, it was not as he expected. Suddenly he came face to face with a truth that he could never have imagined. The enemy, who could not make sense of this action of this hero of Islam and hero of the hearts of people, asked Ali in shock and with great curiosity:

"O Ali! Why did you stop when you were just about to kill me? What brought about this change of mind? What happened that made you go from a violent rage to a remarkable calmness... You were like a bolt of lightning about to strike before you suddenly calmed down..."

Ali replied:

"I use this sword of the Prophet in the path of Allah only. I never let my *nafs* interfere... When you spat on my face you wished to anger and insult me. If I had succumbed to my anger at that point I would have killed you for the base reason of giving in to my own whims, which is something that does not befit a believer. Whereas I fight for the sake of Allah, and not for the satisfaction of my pride".

As a result the heart of that enemy found life again in response to the lofty, praiseworthy character of the person he had come to kill. He took heed from Ali's faith, his sincerity and his opposition to his own desires. The man subsequently became Muslim.

❁

One time a great fire broke out in the copper markets of Baghdad. Two children were trapped in one of the burning shops. Despite their cries for help, the flames were so intense that nobody was brave enough to try and save them. Their foreman was crying out outside in desperation:

"I will give 1000 pieces of gold to whoever saves my children".

At that point Abu'l Hussain Nuri who happened to be passing by, immediately threw himself into the fire. The fire became like a rose garden for him. With the help of almighty Allah, this saint was able to save the children from those flames, to the amazement of everyone watching.

Happily the foreman presented the gold pieces to Abu'l Hussain Nuri, who suddenly grimaced and said:

"Take your gold and be grateful to Allah Most High! If I had done what I did not for Allah but for the hope of some material reward, I would never have been able to rescue those children from that fire".

As can be seen from this example, many fires can become rose gardens with the blessings of sincerity. But to enter the fire is possible only when one becomes like Abraham, the friend of Allah. Because the lack of fear displayed by Abraham in the face of the fire was an exceptional favour that almighty Allah bestowed upon him in response to his submission out of his love and passion for Allah.

❁

Sincerity shows its effect in everything. As long as it is given out with a sincere intention, the one who gives charity will be rewarded to the degree of their sincerity, even if the charity goes to one who is unworthy of it. According to the degree of one's sincerity there arise positive tendencies towards goodness in those who are given the charity. The Messenger of Allah ﷺ has indicated this truth as follows:

"One time a man said: "I am going to give charity".

That night he left his home with his charity and placed it in the hands of a thief without realising who it was. The next day the people of the town started to talk:

"What an amazing thing! Last night someone gave charity to a thief!"

The man said:

"O Allah! Praise be to you. I am going to give charity today as well".

Again he left his home with his money and this time without realising it, he placed it in the hands of a prostitute. The next day the people of the town began to talk once more:

"It cannot be! Last night somebody gave charity to a prostitute".
The man said again:

"O Allah! Praise be to you even if I have given charity to a prostitute. I am going to give charity again".

Again that night, the man took what he had set aside for charity and left his house, this time placing it in the hands of a rich man. The next day the people of the town began to chatter again in amazement:

"What is this! Last night charity was given to a rich man!".

The man said:

"O Allah! I am grateful to you for being able to give charity whether it be to a thief, a prostitute or a rich man.

As a result of the sincerity of this man, he saw someone in his dream say to him:

"Perhaps the charity you gave to the thief will embarrass him and stop him from stealing. And perchance the prostitute will regret what she had been doing and become a chaste woman. And maybe the rich man will take heed and give out to the needy from the wealth that Allah has given him". (Bukhari, Zekat, 14)

And so these are the blessings of sincerity and true devotion... What is indicated in this *hadith* is the necessary sincerity and devotion that needs to be within the heart of the person who is giving charity. It also expresses the idea that intentions are better than deeds. However, let it not be assumed from this that it is a virtuous act to give out charity carelessly. On the contrary, when giving out charity and alms-giving, the believer should give it to those who are truly in need, and must search out the most worthy person if possible and give it to them.

What an admonition is the following event which is a practical demonstration of the above-mentioned hadith.

During a trip to Anatolia by Shaykh Sami Ramazanoglu, somebody stopped his car in Urgup and asked for money to buy some cigarettes. Despite the objections - not voiced, but felt in the hearts - of some of his fellow travellers, Shaykh Sami, who was an ocean of generosity, said:

"Since he is asking, [it is only right that] we should give" and to the surprised looks of those around him he gave him the money without hesitation. Being pleased at this, the poor man changed his intention and said:

"Now I am going to go and buy bread with this money" and he left to go.

This is an evident example of the manifestation of goodness that arises as a result of the degree of the purity of one's intentions and the legitimate and pure source of one's wealth.

❁

During the first years in the history of Islam an unknown person used to leave a sack of provisions every morning at the door of various poor people in Madina. It so happened that one morning the poor people woke up to find that there was no sack at their door. While they were wondering the reason they heard a poignant proclamation of the death of the grandson of Ali ﷺ, Zayn-al-abideen. The city of Madina was shaken up with this news and its people were deeply grieved.

The last duties began to be meticulously carried out for this heir of the Prophet. When it came time to wash his body, the person who performed the task saw some large boils on the back of the dead man. He was surprised and could not understand the reason. Somebody from the *ahl'ul bayt* [14] who knew his secret explained:

---

14. The ahl'ul bayt are the family of the Prophet (translator's note).

"Every morning Zayn-al-abideen would carry sacks of provisions that he had prepared and take them to the doors of the poor. He would return without anyone seeing him. Nobody ever knew who it was that kept bringing these provisions. These wounds that you see on his back are what developed as a result of carrying them". (Ibn-i Kathir, al-Bidaya, IX, 112,133; Abu Nuaym, Hilye, III, 136)

This is the manifestation of sincerity in the heart of a believer full of compassion. This is a sensitivity observed for a lifetime that refused to tarnish the reward for goodness with the compliments of mere mortals.

✻

The following is another beautiful example of sincerity displayed by Sultan Alparslan whose heart was ever together with his Lord.

Before entering the Battle of Malazgirt in 1071, Alparlsan donned pure white clothes and remarked: "This is my shroud". In other words, he had prepared himself not for worldly fame but for martyrdom with the ecstasy resulting from pure faith. Before he went to battle he gave this short speech to his soldiers:

"Either I become victorious and reach my aim; or I become a martyr and go to heaven. Those of you who choose to follow me, let them do so. Those who choose to leave, let them go. There are no commanding sultans giving orders here, nor are there any soldiers needing to obey. Today I am one of you. I am a soldier going to war alongside you. Those who follow me and become martyrs having devoted their souls to almighty Allah - to heaven you go; those left alive will be war heroes. As for those who desert us, it is the fire of the hereafter and disgrace in this world that await them".

As a result of the sincerity of Sultan Alparslan, almighty Allah made him victorious against the Roman Diyogen, whose army was five times the size of his own.

As mentioned before only those people who possess sincerity will attain to true salvation. However the possessors of sincerity are in great danger constantly and face a risky trial. Likewise the assassination attempt on the life of the great commander of Islam, Sultan Alparslan was such a trial. This is what happened:

In the year 1072 after the victory at Malazgirt, Sultan Alparslan went on an expedition towards Maveraunnehir. He had many horses with him. He besieged the Fortress of Hana which was on the River of Amuderya. The commander of the fortress was Yusuf al-Harazmi who was a member of a heretic group called *Batiniyye*. When he realised that the fortress was not going to be able to hold out much longer, he informed Alparslan that he had surrendered. However when this treacherous villain was brought before Alparslan he suddenly charged at him and wounded him with his dagger. He was immediately killed and Sultan Alparslan was also not to recover from his wounds. He was reunited with his Lord on the 25th of October, 1072. His last words were as follows:

"Whenever I was resolved against the enemy I would always seek refuge in Allah Most High and ask for His help. Yesterday when I climbed a mountain, it was as if the mountain beneath my feet shook due to the number of my soldiers and the greatness of my army. In my heart the following thought arose: "I am the ruler of the world, who can defeat me?" As a result of this, Almighty Allah punished me using one of His feeble servants. I ask Allah Most High for forgiveness for this thought that arose in my heart and for all of the mistakes and errors that I have committed in the past, and I turn back to Him. There is no Allah but Allah and Muhammad is the Messenger of Allah..."

Undoubtedly this state is that of a sincere conscience and a pure heart taking itself to account.

❋

One of the friends of Allah was once asked if he had ever experienced any event concerning sincerity that had left an impression on him. He replied:

"Indeed I have" and he explained:

"One time I lost my purse at Mecca and was left penniless. I was expecting money from Basra but it had somehow failed to arrive. My hair and beard had grown somewhat. I went to a barber and asked him:

"I have no money. Would you cut my hair for the sake of Allah?"

At that point the barber was shaving a man. Indicating the seat next to him he said: "Sit here" and leaving him he began to shave me. The man objected. The barber turned to him and said:

"I am sorry sir. I was shaving you for a fee but this person here asked me to shave him for the sake of Allah. Duties done for Allah always have priority and they have no fee. The servants can never know the price of those things done for Allah and never can they pay them".

After he shaved me, the barber slipped a few pieces of gold into my pocket:

"You can attend to your immediate needs with this. This is all I have, I am sorry".

A few days passed. The money I was waiting for from Basra arrived. I took a small pouch of gold to the barber but he objected:

"I will never take it! None of the slaves of Allah can ever have the ability to pay the price for a task done for Allah's sake. Be on your way. May Allah give you peace".

I made amends and parted from him but for forty years now I have been waking up in the middle of the night and praying for him".

And so almighty Allah will reward those righteous deeds and all acts of goodness with goodness that is worthy of His glory as long as they are done in such a sincere manner, that is purely for the sake of Allah.

❈

During the days of Ramadhan many rich people within the Ottoman community, used to wander around unfamiliar suburbs in uncharacteristic dress. Going to the markets, grocers and shops of the region they would ask them to take out their credit book. They would tell them to add up the debts of some of the pages at random from the beginning, the middle and the last pages. Having totalled them they would pay the resulting amount. They would then leave without identifying themselves saying:

"Clear these debts! And may Allah accept this deed from us".

And so it was that the one in debt never knew who it was that had paid off his debts, and the one who wiped away the debt would never know who it was whom he had saved from debt. Those individuals knew that non-obligatory charity given in secret was more acceptable than that given out in the open and so they tried to help others as secretly as possible. Our forefathers were so sincere that their right hand was unaware of the charity that had been given out by their left hand and they would immediately forget the good that they had done.

The distinguished friends of Allah have advised people to forget two things:

1. The good deeds that you have done so that they do not boost your ego and make you vain and proud;

2. The bad things that have been done to you so that ill-will and rage do not germinate within your heart.

In short, sincerity is a jewel so hard to attain and preserve that no one other than Allah can truly evaluate its worth, because through it the windows of the heart are opened to Allah. Sincerity is a sublime quality that raises a servant to high ranks both in this world and the next and that brings one closer to Allah. Allah Most High does not accept deeds that are done devoid of sincerity. On the Day of Judgement, deeds done with self-satisfaction and for show, both of which indicate diseases of the heart, will be thrown at the faces of the ones who perform them. Sincerity on the other hand makes what is little great, through the bounty of Allah most High. It also makes one's life long and its abundance and prosperity continual.

3. *Taqwa* [15] (Piety and God-consciousness)

Taqwa means protecting the heart from anything other than Allah or anything that distances one from Allah so that the heart becomes a mirror of beautiful manifestations. *Taqwa* is when the believer seeks refuge in the protective security of Allah and meticulously preserves himself from things that will give harm and pain in the hereafter and distances himself from sins in order to embrace good deeds.

---

15. *Taqwa* comes from the root word *waqa'a* which means to guard, preserve, safeguard. It has the meanings of godliness, devoutness and piety (translator's note).

The Prophet Muhammad ﷺ, stated in an address to Abu Dharr ؓ that *taqwa* was the sole standard of any worth and acceptance in the eyes of Allah:

"Know that you are above neither the red person nor the black person. It is only taqwa *that makes you superior"* (Ahmad, V, 158)

The Blessed Prophet ﷺ said:

"I am the most God-fearing amongst you". (Bukhari, Iman, 13; Muslim, Siyam, 74). He acted with the standards of *taqwa* at every stage of his life. This is why it is necessary to comply with the *sunnah* [16] of the Messenger of Allah in order to be a God-fearing believer.

The Prophet Jesus عليه السلام has beautifully described *taqwa* as follows:

Somebody once came to Jesus and asked him:

"O teacher of goodness and righteousness! How does the slave become a possessor of *taqwa* in the sight of Allah Most High?"

Jesus responded:

"Easily. By loving Allah Most High as He deserves to be loved, with your heart and soul, and by performing righteous deeds to the best of your ability in order to please Him, and by showing mercy and compassion to all of the sons of Adam just as you would show for yourself".

Then he said:

"Never do to another what you do not wish to have done to yourself! Then you will be a person who has proper *taqwa* of Allah". (Ahmad, Az-Zuhd pg 59).

---

16. The sunnah are the collection of practices of the Prophet Muhammad (translator's note).

One day Omar ﷺ asked Ubayy bin Ka'b ﷺ to define *taqwa*. Ubayy bin Ka'b answered him:

"O Omar, have you ever walked along a prickly path?"

When Omar answered "Yes I have" he then asked him:

"So what did you do?"

Omar answered:

"I lifted up my garments and concentrated all my efforts into preventing the thorns from harming me".

Upon this Ubayy bin Ka'b said:

"That is *taqwa*" (Ibn-i Kathir, Tafsir"ul Qur'an al Azim, Beirut 1988, I,42).

The essence of *taqwa* is to flee from unbelief and associating partners with Allah as one would flee from fire. The sign of this is that one performs the obligatory tasks properly and refrains from all sin.

The Blessed Prophet ﷺ said:

"*Fear Allah wherever you happen to be, and perform a good deed after a bad one so that it erases it. And behave with good character towards people*" (Tirmidhi, Birr, 55/1987)

The peak of *taqwa* is when the servant protects his heart from everything that will make it heedless of Allah and turns towards Him with his entire being, the degree of which has no limit. This last stage is the true *taqwa* that is commanded in the following verse:

"**O you who have attained to faith. Be conscious of Allah with all the consciousness that is due to Him and do not allow death to overtake you before you have surrendered yourselves unto Him**" (*Al'i Imran, 3: 102*)

In order to reach the peak of *taqwa* one must avoid doubtful things at all costs. The Messenger of Allah ﷺ said:

"The slave of Allah cannot reach a degree of true taqwa *unless he abandons things that are not objectionable out of fear that he may do something objectionable"* (Tirmidhi, Qiyama, 19/2451; ibn-Maja, Zuhd, 24)

Abdullah ibn Omar ﷺ warns us of the following:

"A person cannot attain to a true level of *taqwa* without abandoning the things that make him uncomfortable and that trouble his heart". (Bukhari, Iman, 1)

In order to gain *taqwa* the slave must constantly take his soul to account. This is because it is only possible to strengthen one's *taqwa* by resisting the intense desires of the evil-commanding soul, which is the greatest enemy of the heart, and protecting it from its deceptions.

In order to refrain from falling for all of the formidable allurements that were laid before him, the prophet Joseph عليه السلام showed that the only cure was to seek refuge in Allah with a high degree of *taqwa*. And this shows that *taqwa* is a must if one wishes to engage divine help.

The Prophet Muhammad ﷺ would supplicate to almighty Allah and ask for *taqwa* to be bestowed upon him:

"O Allah! Grant piety to my soul, purify it as Thou art the best to purify it and Thou art its Guardian and Master". (Muslim, Zikr, 73)

"O Allah! I ask you for guidance, piety, chastity and wealth of the heart". (Muslim, Zikr, 72)

The most superior person in the eyes of Allah is the one who possesses the greatest degree of *taqwa* or piety[17]. Allah Most High

---

17. See al Hujurat, verse 13

loves his pious servants[18] and is always with them[19]. He has promised the pious ones Paradise as wide as the heavens and the earth[20]. Almighty Allah bestows upon his pious slaves the ability to distinguish between good and bad and He forgives their sins[21]. He shows them a way out in moments of distress and provides for them from where they would never have expected. He makes their task easy, forgives their evil and grants them great reward[22].

According to a narration by Abu Darr ﷺ the Messenger of Allah ﷺ said:

"I know a verse. If people held tight to it, it would be enough for them".

His Companions asked him:

"What is that verse, o Messenger of Allah?"

Allah's Messenger recited the following from the Holy Qur'an:

"...Whoever has taqwa of Allah – He will facilitate for him a way out" (Talaq, 65: 2) (ibn Majah, Zuhd, 24)

Those who have piety are the ones who are closest to the Prophet spiritually. Muadh bin Jabal ﷺ states the following:

"When the Messenger of Allah ﷺ sent me to Yemen as governor, he escorted me all the way to the outskirts of Madina to bid farewell to me. I was on my mount while he was walking. After he had given me some advice he said:

"O Muadh! It may be that you will not see me again after this year. It is possible that when you next come to visit this mosque of mine you will find my tomb in its place".

---

18. See Al'i Imran, verse 76
19. See an Nahl, verse 128
20. See Al'i Imran, verse 133
21. See Al Anfal, verse 29
22. See al Talak, verse 2-5

Hearing these words I started to cry out of the sorrow that comes from parting from a friend such as the Messenger of Allah ﷺ. The Messenger of Allah said:

"Do not cry o Muadh!". And then turning his face to Madina, he said:

"Those who are closest to me are those who have piety before Allah wherever they happen to be" (Ahmad, V, 235. Haysami, Majmua'z-Zawaid, Beirut, 1988, IX, 22)

The Prophet also said:

"Undoubtedly my friends are the pious ones". (Abu Dawud, Fiten, I/4242).

A heart that has attained to *taqwa* is honoured with being under the providence of the Divine, and becomes the site of the manifestation of divine wisdom and mysteries.

Scenes of Virtue

The true scholars and friends of Allah such as Abu Hanifa, Imam Shafii, Ahmad bin Hanbal lived their lives with the standard of *taqwa*. One time as Imam Abu Hanifa was trying to clean a tiny stain on his garment, he was asked:

"O Imam! According to a *fatwa*[23] you have given, this tiny stain is not an obstacle to the prayer; so why are you trying so hard to remove it?"

Abu Hanifa replied:

"That is *fatwa*, this, on the other hand, is *taqwa*"...

---

23. A *fatwa* is a legal ruling regarding the practices of Islam given by a qualified scholar (translator's note).

As can be seen *taqwa* is to display the greatest degree of meticulousness and care in the face of Allah's commands and prohibitions.

❈

The following story is very telling in showing the piety of a woman who, when she spoke, spoke nothing but verses from the Qur'an out of fear of falling into sin:

Abdullah bin Mubarak narrates:

One time I had set out with the aim of performing the *hajj* at Allah's Sacred House, the *Kabah* and visiting the tomb of the Prophet 變, when I saw something black in the middle of the road. I looked carefully and saw that it was a woman with a cloak made of wool on her back and a veil of wool over her head... I greeted her:

"*Salamu alaykum wa rahmetullahi wa barakatuhu* (May the peace, mercy and blessings of Allah be upon you)".

She replied from chapter Yasin of the Qur'an:

"Peace!" A word from a Merciful Lord".

"May Allah bring you good! What are you doing here?" he I asked.

She replied with the 186th verse of Chapter A'raf:

"If Allah misguides people, no one can guide them".

I realised that she had lost her way. So I asked her:

"Where do you want to go?"

She replied with a portion of the first verse of Chapter Isra:

"Glory be to Him who took His slave on a journey by night from the Masjid al-Haram to the Masjid al-Aqsa".

I understood that she had made the pilgrimage and wanted to go to Jerusalem. I asked her:

"How many days have you been here?

She replied with the 10th verse of Chapter Mariam:

"For three nights despite the fact that you are perfectly able".

"Don't you have anything to eat" I asked her

She read the 79th verse of the chapter Shu'ara:

"He who gives me food and gives me drink".

"How can you perform the ablution in this dry desert?" I asked her

She replied with the 43rd verse of Chapter Nisa:

"(If) you cannot find any water, then do *tayammum*[24] [cleanse yourself] with pure earth".

"I have something to eat with me. Would you like to eat?" I asked. She responded with a part of the 187th verse of chapter Baqara:

"...then fulfil the fast until the night appears".

"This is not the month of Ramadan" I said. She answered with a portion of the 158th verse of chapter Baqara:

"If anyone spontaneously does good, Allah is All-Thankful, All-Knowing".

---

24. *Tayyammum* is a form of purification in cases where no water is available. It is performed by wiping one's hands and face over clean earth, or some similar substance (translator's note).

"To break the fast is permissible when you are on a journey" I said. She responded with a part of the 184th verse of chapter Baqara:

"But that you should fast is better for you, if you only knew".

"Why don't you speak to me in the way that I am speaking to you?" I asked her. She answered by reading the 18th verse of chapter Qaf:

"He does not utter a single word, without a watcher by him, pen in hand!"

"Shall I let you mount my camel and take you to your tribe" I asked her. She replied with a portion of verse 197 from chapter Baqara:

"Whatever good you do, Allah knows it".

I got my camel ready for her to mount it. She read a part of the 30th verse of chapter Nur:

"Say to the believers that they should lower their eyes".

While she climbed up onto the camel, she read a portion of the 13th and 14th verses of chapter Zuhruf:

"Glory be to Him who has subjected this to us. We could never have done it by ourselves".

When we started moving she read from the 20th verse of Chapter Muzemmil:

"Recite as much of the Qur'an as is easy for you".

Inspired by the 269th verse of chapter Baqara I then said:

"He who has been given wisdom has been given great good".

I said to her:

"You have been given much good". She finished this verse:

"But no one pays heed but people of intelligence".

At last we reached her caravan.

"Here is your caravan. Who do you have in it?" I asked

She read from the 46th verse of Chapter Kahf:

"Wealth and sons are the embellishment of the life of this world".

I understood that she had sons in the group. I asked:

"What is their role in the pilgrimage group?

She read the 16th verse of chapter Nahl:

"As well as other means of orientation; for it is by the stars that men find their way".

I understood that her sons were the guides of the caravan. Indicating the tents and I asked her:

"Which of them are your sons? She answered:

"Allah took Ibrahim as an intimate friend, and Allah spoke directly to Musa. Yahya, take hold of the Book with vigour".

I then shouted to the caravan:

"O Ibrahim, O Musa, O Yahya". Three young men radiant as the moon came out. When they came and sat down, their mother recited to them from the 9th verse of Chapter Kahf:

"Send one of your number into the city with this silver you have, so he can see which food is purest and bring you some of it to eat". (Kahf, 50:19)

One of the young men went to purchase something to eat and placed it in front of them. The women read the following verse from Chapter Haqqa:

"Eat and drink with relish for what you did before in days gone by!" (69:24)

I said to the sons of the woman:

"May your food be unlawful for me if you do not inform me of your mother's state".

Upon this the young men said:

"For 40 years now, this here our mother has spoken nothing but verses from the Qur'an out of fear of falling into error before Allah, the Most Merciful".

I then read from Chapter Jumu'ah:

"That is Allah's favour which He gives to whoever He wills. Allah's favour is indeed immense" (62:4)

❊

A requirement of *taqwa* is that one abandons that which is doubtful and even lawful, out of fear that one may commit the unlawful. An example of this is as follows:

Sultan Abdulaziz Han, who brought his army and its fleet to a highly impressive rank, obliterating internal conflicts with adept political skill, and who was subsequently able to raise the position of the government to its former prestige, had attracted the attention of the entire world. As a result the Sultan was invited to France and England.

Abdulaziz Han, who was the most religious of sultans, took with him chefs from Bolu, thinking that the food of Europeans would be doubtful under *shariah* (Islamic legal standards).

Abdulaziz Han was a righteous person and led a very religious and ordered life. He had so much piety that throughout his life, he only drank *zamzam*[25] and never drank normal water. He would perform his prayer in the most ordered of fashions and he would read the Qur'an frequently. When he was brutally martyred, a Holy Qur'an opened at the Chapter Joseph, was found on the top of a small table in his room. This Holy Qur'an, which was stained with his blessed blood is preserved in the Topkapi Palace.

It is said in a *hadith* of the Prophet:

"A person dies upon the state that they lived in, and they will be resurrected upon the state that they died"[26].

Another historical personality who lived following highly sensitive standards of *taqwa* was Sultan Abdulhamid II He used to order that he be woken up if anything urgent arose, at whatever time of the night it happened to be, and was never content to leave the task to the following day. His scribe, As'ad Bey, narrates in his memoirs:

"One night at midnight I knocked on the door of the Sultan to ask him to sign a most important document, but he did not open the door. I waited for a while before I knocked once more, but again he did not answer. I became anxious and wondered if the call of Allah had come to the Sultan. I knocked again a little while later and the Sultan appeared at the door with a towel in his hand. He was drying his face. He smiled and said:

"My son! I realised that, at this hour, you must have come for something very important. I had woken up at the very first knock but I was late in answering the door as I went to take my ablution.

---

25. Zamzam is water from a well located in Mecca, found by Hajar, the wife of Abraham (translator's note).
26. See Muslim, Jannah, 83; Munawi, Fayzu"l Qadir, Beirut 1994, V, 663)

This is because I have never signed any document for my people without having first taken my ablution. Bring it to me and let me sign it..." and pronouncing the *Basmala*[27], he signed the document".

The wife of Abdulhamid II narrated the following as an illustration of the degree of his sensitivity:

"Abdulhamid Han always left a clean brick tile at the foot of his bed. When he got out of bed he used to perform *tayammum* with the tile before he went to the basin to perform his ablution with water in order to avoid stepping on the ground without his ablution. One time I asked him the reason for this. He responded as follows:

"As the Caliph of so many Muslims, if I am not careful about the standards of applying the *sunnah,* then the community of Muhammad may be harmed because of this..."

His life of piety made him a genius in the realm of politics too. His foresight has been recorded in world history due to his rule during the most difficult and dangerous of years.

In short, *taqwa* is at the head of those virtues that are the essence of the religion and that beautify one's spiritual life. The greatest capital that one can possess in order to attain to happiness in the next world is *taqwa*. A life without *taqwa* is full of peril. A life that is not lived upon the principles of *taqwa* will result in misfortune at the last breath and thus eternal loss, as is indicated by the *hadith* "*However you live, that is how you will die*". (Munavi, V, 663) – and may Allah protect us. In order to protect ourselves from the evil of our carnal desires in this temporary world, it is

---

27. The *basmala* is the oft-repeated phrase by Muslims uttered before beginning anything and means 'In the Name of Allah, the Most Merciful, the Most Compassionate'

vital that we live as meticulous and careful a life as we would if we were walking through a minefield.

Wars are fought and come to an end at particular times and in particular places. Whereas the struggle for *taqwa* against the evil-commanding soul must continue uninterruptedly for a lifetime. It is stated in a verse from the Qur'an:

"And worship your Lord until what is Certain (death) comes to you". (Hijr, 15:99).

May Almighty Allah bestow upon us a lifelong servanthood based on taqwa and a continued state of vigilance in the face of "heedlessness" which opens up the doors to the trickery and deceptions of our lower self.

Amen

4. Tawba and Istigfar

The human being has a tendency to incline towards sin when it is defeated by the desires of its *nafs* and when it loses the enlightenment of faith and its spirituality. When the moral support from the conscience decreases, discernment and spiritual depth also disappear. A serious weakness appears in the road to becoming a person of integrity. Sins become like sweet music to the *nafs* and are committed without feeling the heaviness of their evil consequences.

Whereas mankind comes to this world immaculately pure, like a clean and clear mirror of innocence. Religion then is a manifestation of mercy bestowed upon mankind by Allah in order to preserve this primal purity. Consequently if a servant has been able to preserve the purity within his nature and benefitted from the spirituality of religion, he will then be able to draw back the veils of heedlessness. This will then allow him to feel the enormity of his sin in his conscience, if he so happens to commit one. Having thus been injured, the virtuous feelings that have been hidden away in his inner world will be awakened. With great sorrow, his heart will burn with regret and he will open it up to his Lord with teary eyes. This burning and regret is called *"tawba"*. The cries for forgiveness that come after and flow from the heart, are termed *"istigfar"*.

Sins are obstacles to entering Paradise; in contrast *tawba* which is strengthened by good deeds and a penitent heart, are means of protection from the fire.

The Prophet Muhammad ﷺ said:

"When a servant commits a sin, a black stain is imprinted upon his heart. If he abandons that sin and embraces istigfar *and inclines towards* tawba, *his heart is then polished. If he does not do so and turns back towards the sin, the black spots increase and consequently cover the entire heart. This is the situation that Allah Most High has mentioned in the Qur'an:*

"No indeed! Rather what they have earned has rusted up their hearts". (Mutaffifin, 83:14) (Tirmidhi, Tafsir, 83/3334)

It has been stated in another hadith:

"The biggest concern of a person is the anxiety of sin; its cure is to do istigfar *in the darkness of the night".* [28]

Whenever one commits a sin, which can happen to everyone as a result of being human, one must immediately repent and ask for forgiveness and turn back towards Allah. Almighty Allah praises his pious servants that he is pleased with as follows:

""Those who, when they act indecently or wrong themselves, remember Allah and ask forgiveness for their bad actions (and

---

28.   Deylemi, al Firdaws bi Me"suri"l Hıtab, Beirut, 1986, I, 136

who can forgive bad actions except Allah?) and do not knowingly persist in what they were doing. (Al'i Imran, 3:135)

"The part of the night they spent asleep was small and they would seek forgiveness before the dawn". (Adh-Dhariyat, 51:17-18)

Almighty Allah informs us in many verses that He will forgive those servants of His who repent with sincerity. In fact, He states that He will transform the sins of those who turn towards him with sincere repentance into good deeds:

"...except for those who make tawba and have faith and act rightly: Allah will transform the wrong actions of such people into good – Allah is Ever-Forgiving, Most Merciful". (Furqan, 25:70)

The Blessed Prophet ﷺ has said:

"Allah Most High, opens up His hands at night time, in order to accept the repentence of those who commit sins by day. And for those who commit sins at night time He opens up His hands during the day. This continues until the sun rises from the place it sets, that is, until the Day of Judgement". (Muslim, Tawba, 31)

The most important condition for *tawba* is sincerity and genuineness. One who continually breaks their *tawba* has obviously become a plaything of Satan. Almighty Allah states:

"Allah's promise is true. So do not let the life of this world delude you and do not let the Deluder delude you concerning Allah". (Luqman, 31:33)

On the other hand, *tawba* and *istigfar* are means to free oneself of pain both in this world and the next. The Messenger of Allah ﷺ stated that:

"With the following verses Allah Most High revealed to me two assurances for my community:

77

1. **Allah would not punish them** (*as a whole*) **while you were among them.**

2. **Allah would not punish them as long as they sought forgiveness.** (anfal, 8:33)

"When I part from them (my community) I leave for them (the second assurance, that is, istigfar which will prevent Allah's punishment and protect them until the Day of Judgement". (Tirmidhi, Tafsir, 8/3082).

Tawba and *istigfar* are two of the most effective means to approaching Allah, because their true nature is that they indicate genuine regret and the seeking of refuge in Allah. *Istigfar*, which has an important place in turning towards Allah and in the heart's gaining an elevated rank, is the unique means to purifying oneself from spiritual blemishes. An acceptable *tawba* will raise the veils and remove the obstacles that lay between the servant and his Lord, and will leave one subject to the love of Allah Most High. As such, almighty Allah states:

"Allah loves those who turn back from wrongdoing and He loves those who purify themselves". (Baqara, 2:222)

The Prophet Muhammad ﷺ gave the following example to describe the pleasure of our Lord when people make *tawba* to Him:

"The pleasure of Allah Most High when any one of you repent from his sins is greater than the pleasure of one who is travelling through the isolated desert and loses his camel which is carrying his food and drink. When all his attempts to find it fail, he loses all hope that he ever will and he lies down under the shade of a tree. Suddenly he sees his camel at his side and he sticks to his halter and, not knowing what to say out of extreme happiness he says:

"O Allah! You are my servant and I am your Lord". (Muslim Tawba 7: Tirmidhi, Qiyamah, 49, Deawat, .99)

In another *hadith*, the Messenger of Allah ﷺ explains the benefits of *istigfar*:

"If a person never abandons asking Allah for forgiveness, Allah Most High will show him a way out of all distress, and freedom from all sadness, and will provide for him from where he would never have expected". (Abu Dawud, Vitir, 26/1518; Ibn-i Maja, Adab, 57)

Thus the most important matter for the servant is to purify his soul and cleanse his heart. What has been explained thus far about *tawba* and *istigfar* are only the beginning of this state. Once one has entered through the door, righteous deeds are a must. After one has performed the obligatory, necessary and *sunnah* deeds in the correct manner, one must also adopt beautiful virtues such as extreme care in guarding others' rights, compliance to the rights of the parents, giving out for the sake of Allah, and seeking nearness to all of creation by showing mercy, compassion and forgiveness towards them.

Scenes of Virtue

The Prophet Muhammad ﷺ stated:

"O people! Repent towards Allah and ask forgiveness from Him. For I make tawba to Him one hundred times a day". (Muslim, Zikir, 42)

The fact that the Messenger of Allah made *tawba* and *istigfar* to Allah continually, even though all of his past and future sins were forgiven, is an important lesson for his community as well as being gratitude for the favours that Allah bestowed upon him.

The Blessed Prophet, who knew that the most vital duty of the slave is to remember Allah and to worship Him at every instant, did *tawba* and embraced *istigfar* at every opportunity believing that he needed to increase the amount of worship he did. He also used to do *tawba* and *istigfar* for his community.

❉

Ibn-i Omar ﷺ states:

We used to hear the Messenger of Allah ﷺ say 100 times in a single sitting:

رَبِّ اغْفِرْ لِى وَتُبْ عَلَيَّ إِنَّكَ أَنْتَ التَّوَّابُ الرَّحِيمُ

"O *Allah! Forgive me and accept my* tawba. *Because You accept* tawba *much and you are very merciful*". (Abu Dawud, Vitir, 26/1516; Tirmidhi, Deawat, 3434)

The *tawba* and *istigfar* carried out by Allah's Messenger were not due to any mistake or fault on his part, but were rather in order to acquire a nearness to Allah Most High and to gain His pleasure. Because the Prophet was in a state of continuous spiritual growth, he would continually make *istigfar* for each previous state and degree.

❉

During his last days, the Messenger of Allah ﷺ would frequently say:

سُبْحَانَ اللّٰهِ وَبِحَمْدِهِ أَسْتَغْفِرُ اللّٰهَ وَأَتُوبُ اِلَيْهِ

"I *absolve Allah of all of those attributes that do not befit the position of divinity and I give praise Him.*

The Prophet's wife, Aisha ﷺ once asked him:

"O Messenger of Allah! I hear you saying these words often. What is the reason for this?"

The Prophet replied:

"My Lord informed me that I would see a sign within my community. Ever since I have seen this sign I have been saying this glorification. I saw that sign in the following verse from chapter Nasr, which points to the conquest of Mecca:

"When Allah's help and victory have arrived and you have seen people entering Allah's religion in droves, then glorify your Lord's praise and ask His forgiveness. He is the Ever-Returning".
(Muslim, Salat, 220).

The Messenger of Allah ﷺ also taught his community different ways of doing istigfar. The most important of these is the *Sayyid'ul Istigfar*, which he explained in the following *hadith*:

"The highest form of *istigfar* is for the slave to say the following:

اَللّٰهُمَّ اَنْتَ رَبِّى لاَاِلٰهَ اِلاَّ اَنْتَ خَلَقْتَنِى وَاَنَا عَبْدُكَ وَاَنَا عَلٰى عَهْدِكَ وَوَعْدِكَ

مَااسْتَطَعْتُ اَعُوذُبِكَ مِنْ شَرِّ مَا صَنَعْتُ اَبُوءُ لَكَ بِنِعْمَتِكَ عَلَىَّ اَبُوءُ ذَنْبِى

فَاغْفِرْلِى فَاِنَّهُ لاَيَغْفِرُ الذُّنُوبَ اِلاَّ اَنْتَ

"O Allah! You are my Lord. There is none worthy of worship but You. You created me. And I am your slave. I will keep my promise that I gave to You from before time immortal to the best of my ability. I seek refuge in You from the evil of the mistakes that I have made. I declare to You in Your presence, and with indebtedness for the favours that you have bestowed on me and I admit my sins. So forgive me, because there is none other who can forgive sins but You".

The Blessed Prophet ﷺ continued:

"Whoever reads this Sayyad'ul istigfar by day with full conviction of the heart of its good rewards and virtues, will be of Paradise if he dies before the night. And whoever reads it at night believing fully in its rewards and virtues, then he will be for Paradise if he dies before the morning". (Bukhari, Dawat, 2, 16; Abu Dawud, Adab, 100-101)

❁

It is necessary to do *tawba* and *istigfar* and then to strengthen them by immediately performing a righteous deed afterwards. Ibn-i Omar ﷺ explains:

"Somebody once came to the Messenger of Allah ﷺ and asked:

"I have committed a great sin. Is there any chance of *tawba* for me?"

The Messenger of Allah asked:

"Is your mother still living?"

The Companion replied "no".

"Well do you have an auntie", he asked.

The Companion replied:

"Yes, I do".

When the Prophet heard this he said:

"In that case treat her well. The maternal auntie is like the mother". (Tirmidhi, Birr, 6; Ahmad, II, 13-14)

Here the Prophet advised his Companion who had been full of regret and carrying out *istigfar* to strengthen his *tawba* with good deeds. He made it known that good deeds and righteous acts can act as penance for bad deeds and thus eliminate them.

❁

One night the Prophet Muhammad saw Bilal ؓ in his dream. The next morning he called Bilal, the muezzin, and said to him:

"Bilal! Last night I heard the clicking of your shoes in front of me. Tell me which it is of your deeds that has taken you to Paradise ahead of me?"

Bilal answered:

"O Messenger of Allah! Whenever I commit a small sin I immediately rise and pray two rounds of the prayer. And whenever I lose my ablution I immediately renew it".

Upon this the Prophet said:

"This is the reason".

Thus whenever we do anything wrong it is necessary for us to make *tawba* without losing time and to embark upon righteous deeds.

❁

Ka'b bin Malik ؓ, who, due to his negligence left it too late to participate in the Tabuk Expedition and who then missed the convoy as a result, immediately made *tawba* and *istigfar* because of his mistake and was so full of regret that the world in all its greatness became a very narrow place for him. When he received news that his *tawba* had been accepted, he immediately prostrated out of happiness. (Ibn'i Majah, Salat, 192). Later, he wished to give out charity and thus entrusted all of his wealth to the Prophet. But the Messenger of Allah advised him to give out half of his wealth and leave the other half for his family. (Bukhari, Megazi, 79).

This is because Allah's Messenger accepted people's charity according to the state of their heart. He did not want them to later regret what they had given out and have their reward diminished.

❁

Almighty Allah delivers from all manner of distress those of His servants who make *tawba* and *istigfar* and bestows upon them many favours. One time, four people came to Hasan al Basri with their complaints. One complained of drought, another of poverty, another about the infertility of his fields, and the last one complained that he had no children. They asked for his help. This great saint advised each of them to do *istigfar*. Those around him said:

"These people's problems and distress were all different and yet you advised them all the same thing". Hasan al-Basri answered them by reciting the following verse from the Qur'an:

"Ask forgiveness of your Lord. Truly He is Endlessly Forgiving. He will send heaven down on you in abundant rain and reinforce you with more wealth and sons, and grant you gardens and grant you waterways. (Noah, 71:10-12) (Ibn-i Hajar, Fethu'l-Bari, XI, 98; Ayni, Umdetu'lKari,Beirut ts. XXII, 277-278)

To delay making *tawba* by succumbing to the temptation of Satan is like wasting one's life which is one of the worst things one can waste. A smart believer should hurry to repent for his sins and prepare himself for the moment of his last breath.

According to certain narrations a tailor once asked a righteous man:

"What do you have to say about the *hadith* of the Messenger of Allah ﷺ which says: *"Allah Most High will accept the tawba of a person while the soul has yet to reach the throat"* (Tirmidhi, Dawat, 98/3537). That righteous man asked the tailor:

"Yes this is true. But tell me, what is your profession?"

"I am a tailor, I sew clothes".

"What is the easiest thing about tailoring?"

"To take my scissors and cut the cloth".

"How long have you been doing this for?"

"For 30 years".

"When your soul reaches your throat will you be able to cut cloth?"

"No I would not".

"O tailor! If you will not be able to do what you have been doing for 30 years with ease and which you struggled with for a while in order to learn to do, then how will you be able to make *tawba* at that moment if you have never done it in your whole life-time? Make *tawba* now while you still have your strength and power! Otherwise forgiveness and a good end may not befall you at your last breath... Haven't you ever been given advice to hurry to make *tawba* before death comes to you". (Munavi, V, 65)?"

Upon this the tailor immediately repented with all sincerity and became a righteous man.

The Prophet informed us that however people live that is how they will die and however they die is how they will be raised up".[29]

❁

Bayazid-i Bistami once came across a doctor who was preparing some medicine. He asked him:

"O doctor! Do you have the cure for my sickness?"

The doctor asked:

"What is your sickness?

"The sickness of sin" he replied.

---

29. See Muslim Jannah, 83 Munavi, V, 663

The doctor lifted his hands to both sides and said:

"I do not know the cure for the sickness of sin".

At that moment an insane young man (majzoob) who happened to be there interrupted:

"I know the cure for your sickness" he said. Bayazid happily said to him:

"Tell me young man".

The young man, whom the people thought was insane but who was in actual fact a true learned person, described the cure for the sickness of sin as follows:

"Take 10 drams of the *tawba* root and 10 leaves of *istigfar*. Put them in the mortar of your heart. Grind them with the pestle of *tawheed*. Sift them through the sieve of fairness. Knead them with your tears. Cook them in the oven of love and remorse. Swallow 5 spoons from the resulting paste every day; and nothing will remain of your illness".

Bayazid'i Bistami who was listening intently, sighed and said:

"Woe to those who think they are clever and call wise ones such as yourself insane".

In short, mankind is not immune from making mistakes and so must always have *tawba* and *istigfar* on their lips. He must also register and reinforce his intention with good deeds. *Istigfar* and good deeds are a necessary requirement of being a slave of Allah. It is said in a verse from the Qur'an:

"Mankind! Allah's promise is true. Do not let the life of this world delude you and do not let the Deluder (Satan) delude you about Allah". (Fatir, 35: 5)

To delay repenting for one's sins to the last part of one's life by following one's *nafs* and Satan, is the biggest deception whose end result will be loss. In that case it is necessary to repent and ask for forgiveness and to be sincere and become upright with good deeds. Just as this state protects one from misfortune and troubles, it also allows one to attain to Divine favours and bounties.

5. Obedience to the commands of Allah and His Messenger

The spiritual degree of a believer is in accordance with the degree to which they obey the commands of Allah and His Messenger. And the perfection of one's faith increases with the degree of the meticulousness, sensitivity, love and ardour within this obedience. Those people who move up a step up in their love and obedience are those who are subject to divine bounties in both worlds. It is stated in a verse from the Qur'an:

"Whoever obeys Allah and the Messenger will be with those whom Allah has blessed: the Prophets and the sincere lovers of truth, the martyrs and the righteous. What excellent company such people are! (Nisa 4:69)

The Messenger of Allah ﷺ has informed us:

"Your Lord – dignified and majestic is He – states: "If my servants obeyed Me in the manner required, I would make the rain pour down for them at night and make the sun rise over them during the day. And I would not let them hear even the roar of thunder". (Ahmad, II, 359; Hakim, IV, 285/7657)

The hearts of those who carry out their obedience to Allah's commands with love and submission and who can preserve their state of contentment under changing conditions, will become conduits of wisdom, goodness and prosperity. In contrast to this, those hearts and bodies which have not been protected from unlawful and doubtful things, will turn into complete refuges of evil and nests of immorality.

Scenes of Virtue

Before embarking on the battle of Badr, Allah's Messenger ﷺ wished to learn the opinion of his Companions. Mikdad bin Aswad ﷺ rose and gave the following speech:

"O Messenger of Allah! Do whatever you have been commanded to do. We are with you. I swear by Allah we will not say to you that which the sons of Israel said to Moses ﷺ. They said: **"...So you and your Lord go and fight. We will stay sitting here".** (Maida 5:24).

I swear by Allah who sent you as a true prophet that even if you make us walk to Birku'l Gimad[30], as long as we are with you we would withstand even greater difficulty. We are always ready to fight the enemy to the end, on your right, and on your left, and in front of you and behind you[31]. (Bukhari, Megazi 4, Tafsir 5/4; Wakidi, I, 48)

After Mikdad spoke Sa'd bin Muadh ﷺ arose:

"O Messenger of Allah! We have believed in you and We have confirmed you. We have born witness that the Qur'an that you brought with you and the *sunnah* are true. We have promised with certainty that we will listen to your every word and obey you. O Messenger of Allah! Do as you wish! I swear by Allah who sent you as a true prophet that if you were to show us that sea and dive into it, we would dive into it together with you, and none of us

---

30. Birku'l Gimad – a place that is five days from Mecca al Mukarrama, near the Red Sea. It is also reported to be the name of a city in Yemen.
31. Ibn-i Mas'ud has said: "I was witness to such a certain word of Mikdad bin Aswad that to be the possessor of those words seemed more pleasing to me than all other worthwhile words that could be equal to it"..." (Bukhari, Megazi, 4, Tafsir, 5/4)

would stay behind. And we will not feel displeasure at your bring-ing us face to face with our enemies tomorrow. To show patience and forbearance during battle and to remain true to loyalty is our trademark. It is hoped that Allah will show you something from us that will brighten your eye. Come o Messenger of Allah, take us towards the bounty of Allah".

Hearing these words of loyalty and submission, the blessed face of the Messenger of Allah filled up with a smile and he made a prayer asking for goodness:

"In that case come and walk with the bounty of Allah. Let it be glad tidings for you, Allah has promised us one of two unspecified groups[32]. By Allah, it is as if I can see now the places where the Quraysh will be defeated on the battlefield..." (Muslim, Jihad, 83; Wakidi, I, 48-49; Ibn-i HIsham, II, 253-254).

How beautifully the words of the Companions registered their love for and obedience of Allah and His Messenger.

❋

Anas narrates the following *hadith* which presents in the best way the sincerity, genuineness, sensitivity and immediacy of the obedience of the Blessed Companions to Allah and His Messenger:

"I was the cup-bearer at Abu Talha's house. I used to serve the visitors and fill their glasses with wine. At that time alcohol sud-denly became prohibited. Allah's Messenger commanded a public crier to announce this prohibition to the people. We heard the news while we were still in the house. Abu Talha said to me:

---

32. One of the two parties that was promised in the seventh verse of Chapter Al Anfal was the Quraysh themselves, that is them being defeated and taken prisoner, and the other was the large caravan of Quraysh coming from Syria.

"Go outside and find out what this cry is about". I went outside and came back, saying:

"It is a public crier crying out: "Beware, beware, alcohol has been prohibited". He turned to me and said:

"In that case take these and pour out all of this alcohol".

From that point on, wine poured into the streets of Madina (Bukhari, Tafsir, 5/11)

These Blessed Companions obeyed the command as soon as heard that alcohol had been prohibited. They did not put forth excuses, and they did not say: Let me just finish what is in my hand and then I will leave it". They did not linger. They were able to pour out all of the alcohol that was in their possession, including what they were drinking at that very instant.

❁

A young man from the tribe of Aslam came to the Prophet and said:

"O Messenger of Allah! I wish to join the troops, however I do not have any equipment necessary for battle".

The Prophet ﷺ said to him:

"*Go to such and such person; he had prepared to go to battle but he got sick*". The young man went to that person and said:

"The Messenger of Allah ﷺ sends greetings of peace and says that you are to give what you have prepared for battle to me". Upon this the man turned to his wife:

"My dear lady! Give everything I had prepared for battle to this young man. Do not leave anything behind. Do not leave anything behind for the right of Allah so that we may be blessed in this". (Muslim, Imare, 134)

This Companion obeyed the command of the Messenger of Allah with great passion and ardour, and insisted that his wife give everything he had prepared leaving none of it behind. In this way he demonstrated his love, devotion and obedience to the Messenger of Allah and also the great desire and enthusiasm he had for performing good deeds.

❋

Ibn-i Omar ﷺ relates:

"On the day of Victory when the Prophet ﷺ entered Mecca, he asked one of the *hajibs*[33] of the Ka'bah, Othman bin Talha ﷺ to bring the key to the Ka'bah.

Othman went to his mother in whose protection was the key. However the woman, who was a pagan, refused to give him the key. Othman said to her:

"By Allah! Either you give me the key or this sword will come out of its sheath".

The woman handed him the key. Othman brought the key to the Messenger of Allah ﷺ. The Prophet opened the door and entered the House of Allah. Usama ﷺ, Bilal ﷺ and Othman ﷺ entered together with him. The Prophet ﷺ stayed in the Ka'bah for a long time before he finally exited. Following him many people raced each other to get inside.

The first person to get inside was Abdullah bin Omar ﷺ. As soon as he entered he found Bilal ﷺ standing behind the door.

---

33. A *hajib* is a person dedicated to the duty of '*hijabe*', which involves such important duties like taking care of the Ka'bah, the safekeeping of the key and its door, the opening of its doors at certain times for visitors, the preservation and maintenance of the Station of Abraham, valuable gifts, and the inner and outer covers.

"Where did the Messenger of Allah 🕮 pray? He asked. Bilal pointed to the place where the Prophet prayed. Abdullah later said:

"I forgot to ask how many cycles he prayed". (Bukhari, 127, Salat 30, 81, 96, Tahajjud 25, Hajj 51, 52, Megazi 77, 48; Muslim, Hajj 389)

In this example we witness the determination of Othman 🕮 in obeying the command of the Messenger of Allah, and the praiseworthy meticulousness in following the Prophet by Abdullah bin Omar.

❈

The Prophet said:

"Let no one make another person arise from where they are sitting and sit down in his space. Enlarge the circle and make room so that Allah will give you increase".

When Abdullah bin Omar 🕮 learnt of this command of the Messenger of Allah, he applied it his entire life and if someone happened to rise and give him his spot, he never sat there. (Bukhari, Isti'zan, 32; Muslim, Salam, 29)

❈

The Messenger of Allah 🕮 said:

"When you are invited somewhere, accept the invitation".

When Ibn-i Omar 🕮 heard this, he made sure to accept all invitations, to weddings or otherwise, even if he were fasting. (Bukhari, Nikah 71, 74; Muslim, Nikah 103).

That is, if he were performing a supererogatory fast he would break it and then make it up later. If his fast was an obligatory or necessary one, he would still attend the invitation without breaking his fast, in order to comply to the command of the Messenger of Allah 🕮.

❈

The Prophet Muhammad ﷺ one day allocated one of the doors of the Mosque for the ladies. Hearing this, Ibn-i Omar ؓ never again went through that door until the day he died. (Abu Dawud, Salat, 53/571)

❋

Tufay, the son of Ubayy bin Ka'b ؓ, is considered to be of the *Tabi'een*[34]. He used to meet with the Companions and benefit from their knowledge. From time to time he would visit Abdullah bin Omar ؓ and go to the market together with him.

Tufayl explains the meticulousness in the obedience of Abdullah to the commands of the Prophet:

"Whenever we went to the market, Abdullah bin Omar would give greetings of peace to everyone he came across. Whether it be someone who was selling used goods or valuable goods, poor or unknown, he would make sure to greet them all. One day I had gone to see him again. He suggested once more that we go to the market together:

"What are you going to do at the markets?" I asked him. "You know nothing about buying and selling. You don't ask the price of anything you buy. You never buy anything anyway. You don't sit where all the people sit and talk. Instead of going to the market let's sit here and talk".

Hearing this Abdullah ؓ said to me:

"My brother! We are going to the market to give the greeting of *salam* (peace) of Allah to the people we come across. We have no aim other than this". (Muwatta, Salam, 6; Bukhari, al-adab'ul Mufrad, s 348)

---

34. The Tabi'een are the second generation of Muslims after the Companions. They are those Muslims who saw the Companions, but not the Prophet, during their lifetime (translator's note)

All of the Blessed Companions showed the utmost sensitivity in obeying the commands of Allah and His Messenger. By spreading peace amongst the people and increasing love, they fostered an exceptional foundation upon which the brotherhood of faith could be lived in the hearts of the believers. The enthusiasm and fervour of Abdullah bin Omar 🙵 on this topic attracted much attention due to its exalted nature. The above examples show this in a most evident form.

❁

One day the following verse from the Holy Qur'an was revealed: "**You who have faith! Do not raise your voices above the voice of the Prophet**..." (Hujurat, 49: 2)

When Thabit bin Kays 🙵 heard this verse, he sat in his home and wept.

When the Messenger of Allah 🙵 failed to see Thabit for a while, he asked where he was. A person there told him:

"O Messenger of Allah! I know where he is". He went straight to his house and found him, head hung forth, crying.

"What is wrong? Why are you crying?" he asked.

"(Don't ask). I have committed much evil. I have raised my voice above the voice of The Messenger of Allah. All my deeds have been in vain. I am destined for the fire", he answered.

The Companion reported the words of Thabit back to the Prophet. The Prophet said:

"*Go and tell him that he is not for the fire but rather he is for Paradise*". (Bukhari, Menakib, 25, Tafsir 49/1; Muslim, Iman 187).

Thabit, who had a naturally loud voice, was devastated and grief-stricken, thinking that he had disobeyed a command of Allah. However, because his loud voice was a part of his nature and because he had a sincere heart, his situation was an exception and the Companion who brought him the news returned to him in joy at giving him the glad tidings of paradise.

The Companion who had gone to learn the condition of Thabit was also a beautiful example of how the Blessed Companions took any and all indications of the Prophet as commands and were ready to sacrifice their all for him.

❁

The wife of Abdullah bin Rawaha ❧ narrates:

"The Messenger of Allah ❧ had climbed the pulpit (to give his sermon). At the same time Abdullah ❧ was coming towards the Masjid when he heard the call from afar from the Messenger of Allah to "sit". Even though he had not even reached the Mosque, he immediately sat down where he was. When this situation was relayed to the Messenger of Allah ❧ he said to Abdullah:

"May Allah Most High increase the zeal in your obedience for Allah and His Messenger".

❁

Abdullah bin Abbas ❧ narrates:

"Uyayna bin Hisn once came to Madina to visit his nephew Hur bin Kays ❧. Hur bin Kays was one of the members of the advisory committee of Omar ❧. Whether they be young or old, all scholars were included in this advisory committee. For this reason Uyayna said to his nephew, Hur bin Kays:

"My nephew, your standing with the ruler of the government is high. Arrange a meeting for me with him".

Hur asked permission from Omar ❧. When Uyayna entered the presence of Omar he said to him:

"O son of Khattab! I swear by Allah that you do not give us much and you do not rule with justice amongst us".

Omar got angry and wanted to punish Uyayna. Hur, who sensed this, immediately interjected:

"O Commander of the believers! Remember what Allah said to the Prophet – "**Make allowances for people, command what is right, and turn away from the ignorant**". (Araf, 7:199). My uncle is of the ignorant ones".

I swear by Allah that when Hur read this verse Omar immediately changed his mind about punishing Uyayna. Omar was ever devoted to the book of Allah. (Bukhari, Tafsir 7/5, I'tisam 2)

When reminded of a command of Allah, Omar immediately took control of his anger. He obeyed within an instant the divine command and abandoned that which he had wished to do himself. In this way he displayed the sensitivity of a perfect believer when it came to obeying Allah's commands.

❋

Hisham bin Hakim ☙, one of the Companions, was once in Palestine. He saw a group of non-Muslim farmers who had been imprisoned for not paying their taxes and who were being punished by having olive oil poured over them and left to wait under the sun. He went straight to the governor and told him that this was a very bad thing to do. Then he narrated to him a *hadith* that he had heard directly from the Prophet:

"Allah will most definitely inflict pain on those who unrightfully inflict pain on others".

Upon this the governor immediately let the farmers go free. (Muslim, Birr, 117-119; Abu Dawud, Imare, 32; Ahmad III, 403,404,468).

These blessed people did not hesitate, even for a second, in responding to the prophetic announcements, and carried them out immediately.

❀

Abdullah bin Abi Awfa ﷺ had pronounced the *takbir* (*Allahu Akbar*) at the funeral of his daughter four times. After the fourth *takbir*, he paused for the time between the two *takbirs*, and asked that his daughter be forgiven and prayed for her.

Those around him thought that he was then going to make *takbir* for the fifth time. Then he gave his greetings of *salam* to the right and the left. After the prayer they asked him:

"What was this that you just did"?. He replied:

"This is what the Messenger of Allah ﷺ used to do". (Hakim, I, 360; Ibn-i Majah, Janaiz, 24).

The reply of Abdullah bin Abi Awfa ﷺ is very significant in showing the care that the Blessed Companions showed in taking the Prophet of Allah as a model in everything. Their standard was the *sunnah* of the Prophet. This is why all of their defences and explanations were in the form of providing proofs from the Qur'an and the *sunnah*. They organised their life according to the Qur'an and the *sunnah*. And how much we need, today especially, to apply the *sunnah* as our standard in everything we do and to benefit from the prosperity of the Qur'an and *sunnah* so that our proofs and debates can all comply with the divine direction. For the loftiness of our character and personality and the perfection of our Islam is proportional to the degree of our attachment to the Qur'an and the *Sunnah*.

❀

One night when it was time for the *'isha* (nighttime) prayer, the Prophet ﷺ said to his Companions:

"Gather together for the prayer tomorrow. There is something I want to tell you". One of the Companions said to his friends:

"O so and so. You memorise the first thing that the Messenger of Allah says, and then you (o so and so) memorise the second thing, and then (o so and so) you memorise the next so that we do not miss any of what the Messenger of Allah has to say". (Haysami, I, 46).

This care displayed by the Companions in learning and applying the commands of the Blessed Prophet are truly praiseworthy. For it is due to the meticulous efforts of this blessed generation that we have the opportunity today to become closely acquainted with each and every state and action of the Prophet of Allah. May Allah be pleased with them...

❁

Abu Burda narrates:

Once Abu Musa al Ash'ari ﷺ became ill and fainted whilst his head was resting on the lap of his wife. Upon this his wife let out a scream and began to sob loudly. However Abu Musa was not at that time in a position to stop his wife. When he came to, he said to his wife, in the form of a warning:

"Anything that the Messenger of Allah ﷺ was not pleased with and distanced himself from, I am not pleased with and I distance myself from. The Prophet dissociated himself from wailing women who tear their hair out and rip their clothes (out of grief)". (Bukhari, Janaiz, 37, 38; Muslim, Iman, 167; Nesai, Janaiz, 17)

What great sensitivity in faith to try to obey the commands of the Messenger of Allah ﷺ even when grappling with death.

❁

Dihya bin Khalifa 🕮 once saw some people acting contrary to the *sunnah* and he said to them:

"By Allah, I have come face to face with an event which would never have crossed my mind; Certain people have turned away from the *sunnah* of the Prophet 🕮 and His Companions. O Allah! Please take my life now, that I may be with You". (Abu Dawud, Sawm, 47/2413).

❊

Bishr-i Hafi 🕮 states:

"One night I saw the Messenger of Allah in my dream. He said to me:

"O Bishr! Do you know why Allah has increased your worth?"

"No, I do not, o Messenger of Allah" I said. He continued:

"Because you follow my *sunnah*, and you serve the righteous. You advise your brothers in religion, and you love my Companions and the members of my family, and this is why Allah has raised you to the level of the righteous ones[35]".

❊

How beautifully does Abdulhalik Gujduvani 🕮 explain true servanthood:

One day he was asked:

"Should we do what the *nafs* wants us to do, or oppose its demands?"

This saint answered as follows:

---

35. Mahir Iz, Tasawwuf, Istanbul 1969, s. 184)

"It is very difficult to determine the difference between the two of these. The *nafs* generally misleads people as to whether these desires are from Allah, or whether they are from Satan. This is why one should only do what Allah commands and refrain from doing what He forbids. This is true servanthood".

The journeyers on the path of truth must make it an undying principle to obey Allah's commands and to serve and advise their brothers in religion. These are means to eternal happiness and they must be used in the effort to gain Allah's pleasure. One day a person who was a habitual attendant at the talks of David-i Tai said to Maruf-i Kerhi:

"Make sure that you do not abandon good deeds as they will bring you closer to the pleasure of almighty Allah". Maruf asked:

"What deeds should I perform?" That person replied:

"Always be in a state of obedience to your Lord; serve the Muslims and counsel them..."

In short, obedience is the greatest sign of love. There is a principle that "*the one who loves will obey*", and so the believers who love their Lord will always be in a state of obedience to Him. A small act of worship done obediently and submissively is more acceptable in the eyes of Allah than mountains worth of worship done disobediently and unwillingly. This is because servanthood begins with obedience and submission. Satan was cast out of the supreme presence of Allah not because of any deficiency in his worship but rather due to his refusal to obey and submit to the commands of Allah.

The Blessed Companions reached a state of perfection in accordance with the degree of their love for, devotion to and obedience of Allah and His Messenger. By submitting without objection to the divine commands with love and submission, they were able to become model star personalities amongst the entire community.

In his *Mathnawi*, Jalaluddin Al Rumi illustrates nicely the obedience of even lifeless beings to the divine commands:

"Do you not see? The clouds, the sun, the moon and the stars all move about in an orderly fashion. Each of these innumerable stars rises on time. They are never late, nor do they set before their time is due. How is it that we do not understand these wonders by looking at the miracles of the prophets? They gave intelligence to the rock and the staff. See these and then compare those other lifeless beings with the Staff (of Moses) and compare them with other pieces of rock.

The pieces of stone that obeyed the great Prophet Muhammad ﷺ and the obedience of the Staff of Moses to Prophet Moses are an indication of how all other beings that we think are lifeless, in fact bow down to the commands of Allah.

They say through their tongues of disposition: "We know Allah and we obey Him. We are not randomly created things. We each resemble the Red Sea. Even though it was a mere body of water, it was able to recognise the Pharoah that it was about to drown and distinguish him from the sons of Israel...

Wherever it happened to be, a tree or a rock would give greetings of peace to the Prophet Muhammad ﷺ when they saw him; therefore know that everything which you once thought to be lifeless is in actual fact, full of life".

That is, it is not just people and the jinn that are in a state of obedience to Allah and His Messenger, it is also all animals and in fact all non-living things. How sad it is that whilst all creatures are rushing to obey Allah, man is drowning in the pits of rebellion. In that case it is necessary to take heed from the obedience of all creatures created by Allah. We must train ourselves and perfect our conduct before the Divine Presence.

6. Fastidiousness in worship

This universe is like an eternal handiwork of The Divine in which He has embroidered His Greatness and Power. At the centre is man who has been created as the peak of this divine artistry and has been given the duty of worship in order to be assured of being together with Allah.

In many verses in the Qur'an, Almighty Allah commands man to embrace good deeds in order to save himself from eternal loss and to obtain to a sound heart, and a *kalb-i munib*[36].

Worship is a sign of one's loyalty to the promise given by the servant to his Lord before time eternal. They are moments in time which bring the believer closer to Almighty Allah. From another point of view, worship is the most effective cure and source of peace and comfort that will free man of his fear and anxiety about what is to come after death. Worship is an essential source of prosperity in order for the servant to rise in degree and to assure peace and balance of the heart.

Consequently out of all of the matters that we must be extremely careful and sensitive about, our worship must take priority.

Scenes of Virtue

Because of its importance, it is necessary to touch on, first of all, the care that must be shown when taking one's ablution. Because the lack of care and neglect that is shown during the ablution will negatively reflect on the worship that is to follow.

---

36. A *Kalb-i munib* is a heart that ever turns towards Allah with fervour in order to be free of the slavery of ephemeral attractions

One time the Messenger of Allah ﷺ led the morning prayer. Some minor mistakes were made whilst the chapter *Romans* was being recited. After finishing the prayer the Prophet turned to the congregation and said:

"Some people are coming to the prayer without ablution and this is the cause for Satan interfering in our recitation. When you come for prayer, take your ablution as carefully as you can".

Thus purification and the taking of ablution with care before prayer is crucial for the soundness of our worship.

It is also a great virtue to be always in a state of ablution to the best of one's ability. The Messenger of Allah ﷺ liked to carry out all of his tasks while he had ablution.

According to Abu Juhaym ﷺ, the Messenger of Allah ﷺ once came across someone as he was coming from the Well of Jamal. The man greeted him, but the Prophet did not return the greeting. He immediately went to a wall and wiped his hands and face over it to perform the *tayammum* (dry ablution), and then he accepted the man's greeting of peace. (Bukhari, tayammum, 3)

With this action, the Prophet of Allah demonstrated how it is possible for one to always be in a state of ablution. This is also an indication of how virtuous it is to take ablution before carrying out a task, even though that task is not obligatory.

❋

Ibn-i Abbas ﷺ narrates:

"When the Prophet of Allah ﷺ finished relieving himself he would first pour water over his hands to wash them and then he would perform *tayammum* with dry earth. I once asked him:

"O Messenger of Allah, there is water available. Why did you do that?" The Prophet replied:

"How can I be sure that my spirit will not be taken back from me before I reach water?" (Ahmad, I, 288, 303; Haysami, 263).

According to another narration whenever he needed to perform the major ablution, the Prophet ﷺ would wipe his hands over the walls and do *tayammum* in order not to be without ablution until he could perform his major ablution. (Haysami, I, 264).

This is the scope of the material and spiritual cleanliness that the Prophet demonstrated to his community...

❁

One day the Messenger of Allah ﷺ went together with his Companions to a graveyard and said:

"May the peace of Allah be upon you o dwellers of the abode of Believers! Allah willing we will one day join you. How I wish to see my brothers. How much I have missed them".

His Companions asked:

"Are we not your brothers o Messenger of Allah!"

The Prophet replied:

"You are my Companions. My brothers are those who have not yet arrived in this world".

His Companions then asked:

"How will you recognise those who have not yet come as from your community o Messenger of Allah?".

The Prophet ﷺ said:

"Consider a man who has a horse whose forehead and feet are pure white. Would this man not be able to recognise his horse from a herd of other horses, all of which are pitch black?"

His Companions answered:

"Yes he would o Messenger of Allah". Then the Blessed Messenger 🌺 said:

"And so my brothers are those who will come with faces radiant from their ablution and hands and feet shining. I will be waiting for them at the head of my fountain ready to offer them what they desire. But beware! Some people will be cast out of my pool like a wild camel is thrown out of a herd and distanced. I will call out to them:

"Come here". It will be said to me:

"They changed after you left. (They did not follow your sunnah *and strayed far from it)". Then I will say:*

"Let them be distant from me. Let them be distant". (Muslim, Taharat 39, Fedail 26).

Thus those believers who are careful about their ablution will be subject to the love of Allah's Messenger and will be those whom he will address as his 'brothers'. Those who are careless in their ablution and other worship and who deviate towards the wrong path will be cast out like wild camels on the Day of Judgement. They will be afflicted with the most terrible of misfortunes, namely that of being distanced from the Messenger of Allah.

❋

Abu Hazim, from the Tabieen once saw Abu Hurayra 🌺 taking his ablution and washing his arms right up until his armpits.

"Abu Hurayra, what sort of ablution is this?" He asked. Abu Hurayra 🌺 replied:

"O Bani Ferruh! I did not know that you were here? Had I have known that you were here I would not have taken my ablution like this".

He continued by way of explanation:

"I heard my friend, the Messenger of Allah ﷺ say:

"On the Day of Judgement, the light of the believers will reach as far as their water for ablution reached". (Muslim, Taharat, 40)

❋

How beautifully the following words of Ali ﷺ express the love of the Messenger of Allah for his worship:

"On the day of Badr, there was no horseman left other than Mikdad. I remember well that day that everyone slept except for the Messenger of Allah who performed the prayer under a tree and cried until the morning". [37]

This is an example of love of worship that never diminished, neither under conditions of peace nor war...

Almighty Allah states:

"And worship your Lord until what is Certain (death) comes to you". (Hijr, 15:99)

"Prostrate and draw near". (Alaq, 96:19)

❋

The Messenger of Allah ﷺ would praise Abdullah bin Rawaha ﷺ who showed meticulousness in his prayer and he complimented him by calling him 'my brother':

"May Allah have mercy on my brother, Abdullah bin Rawaha! Wherever the time for prayer comes he immediately stands and prays". (Haysami, IX, 316)

❋

Jarh bin Abdullah ﷺ narrates:

---

37. Ibn-i Huzayma, Sahih, Beirut 1970, II, 52

"One night we were sitting with the Messenger of Allah. He looked at the full moon and said:

"Just as you can see that full moon easily, without having to push and shove each other, so too you will be able to see your Lord. Make every effort to perform all of your prayers before the rising of the sun and before its setting".

After that he recited the following verse:

"...glorify your Lord with praise before the rising of the sun and before its setting. And glorify Him during part of the night and at both ends of the day, so that hopefully you will be pleased". (Taha, 20:130)   (Bukhari, Mawakit 16,26, Tafsir 50/1, Tawheed 24; Muslim, Masajid 211).

Thus the greatest means to see our Lord is to show the utmost fastidiousness in performing the prayer.

❋

Every act of worship that is carried out should be seen as an entry visa to Paradise and should be performed with care and with the enthusiasm of the loftiest spirit.

The Prophet 🕌 said:

"If a person performs his prayer in the best way by bowing down and prostrating properly then the prayer will say to that person:

"May Allah preserve you, just as you have preserved me. Prayer raises one's rank.

If a person does not perform their prayer in the best way and does not bow down and prostate properly then the prayer says to him:

107

"May Allah waste you just as you have wasted me". The prayer will be crumpled up like an old piece of clothing and thrown back into his face".[38]

It is stated in a verse from the Qur'an:

"So woe to those who do salat, and are forgetful of their salat". (Maun, 107:4-5)

It is a dire trait to delay the prayer until the last minute and then get up to pray unwillingly as if to get something over and done with and just pray the obligatory part of the prayer. It is so grave that it can lead one to hypocrisy, Allah forbid. Ala bin Abdurrahman ﷺ narrates:

"One afternoon we went to see Anas bin Malik ﷺ. When we arrived Anas immediately rose and prayed the afternoon prayer. After he had finished we told him that he had prayed the prayer early. He explained why he had performed the prayer early:

"I heard the Messenger of Allah say:

"This is the prayer of the hypocrites. This is the prayer of the hypocrites. This is the prayer of the hypocrites[39]. *One of them sits and sits and then just when the sun has turned orange and it is about to set, when the sun enters in between Satan's two horns, he gets up and rises and bows down four times quickly as if he is a pecking hen. He remembers Allah little during his prayer".* (Muwatta, Qur'an al Kareem, 46; Muslim, Masajid 195)

Omar ﷺ once advised his governors as follows:

---

38. Suyuti, Al Jamiu"s Sagir, Egypt 1321,I,58/364
39. This hypocrisy that is mentioned in this hadith is a hypocrisy of action not of belief.

"Your most important duty for me is the prayer. Whoever preserves it and is careful about its times, will preserve his religion and whoever does not perform it and wastes it will lose their religion in a very short time". (Muwatta, Wukut's salat, 6)

✤

Miswar bin Mahrama 🙵 narrates:

"When Omar bin Khattab 🙵 was stabbed he fainted and lay unconsciously. One time I entered the room to visit him. They had covered him and he was lying down. I asked those around him:

"How is he?"

"As you can see, he is unconscious", they answered.

"Have you called him for prayer? If he is alive nothing else can scare and wake him other than the prayer". Upon hearing this they said:

"O Commander of the believers! The prayer, the prayer has been prayed. Omar woke up and said:

"Is that so? By Allah, the one who abandons the prayer will have nothing of Islam". He rose and performed his prayer while the blood from his wounds flowed". (Haysami, I, 295; Ibn-i Sa'd, III, 35; Muwatta, Taharet, 51)

✤

While giving the sermon in Kufa, Ali 🙵 repeated what he had heard from the Messenger of Allah 🙵:

"On Fridays, Satan goes early to the shops and markets and tries to hinder people using a thousand and one obstacles. (If he fails here) he at least tries to delay them from going to the congregational prayer. The angels on the other hand go early to the mosques and wait at the doors. They record those who arrive as

109

follows: those who came in the first hour, then those who came in the second hour, etc. This condition continues until the imam ascends the pulpit. If a person sits down in a spot where he can see and hear the imam and listens with all ears and does not speak, then a twofold reward is written down for him. However if a person sits far away in a place where he cannot hear the imam, and if he remains silent and does not speak, one reward is written down for him. If, however a person sits where he can see the imam but speaks idly and does not remain silent he has two sins recorded for him... (Abu Dawud, Salat, 209/1051).

Those who come early to the mosque out of respect for the Friday prayer and sit where they can comfortably hear the imam and listen and reflect upon what is being said and who are in a state of deep reverence will certainly come out more profitable than those who do not.

❋

One of the leading scholars on commentary and recitation of the Qur'an from the *Tabieen*, Mujahid ﷺ says:

"Abdullah bin Zubayr ﷺ had reached the peak in his worship of Allah, which no one else had reached. One time the area around the Ka'bah where people would walk around was flooded and the people were unable to make *tawaf* of the Ka'bah for a week. Abdullah, on the other hand, made *tawaf* of the Ka'bah for a week by swimming around it. (Ali al Muttaki, XIII, 471/37228; Zahabi, Sier, III, 370).

❋

In his work called *Gulistan,* Shaykh Sadi expresses well the importance of not extinguishing one's worship with mistakes of the heart:

"When I was a child I was very keen on withdrawing from the world and night worship. One night I was sitting next to my father. I had not closed my eyes the whole night and had not put the Qur'an down. Some people around me were sleeping. I said to my father:

"Not one of these people is lifting their heads to pray two cycles of night prayer; they are sleeping as if they are dead". Hearing my words my father furrowed his brow and replied:

"My son Sadi! Would that you had gone to sleep too instead of gossiping about others. (Because even though those whom you are looking down upon right now are probably being deprived of divine mercy, at least the angels are not writing down anything negative about them. But what has been written in your book of deeds? That you belittled your brothers in religion and you committed the sin of gossiping".

❋

The Muslims maintained the fastidiousness they showed in their worship even at times of battle and were consequently subject to the help of Allah. Travijani of Venice describes the brave and victorious army of Yildirim Bayazid as follows:

"There is no wine, gambling or women in the Ottoman army like there is in ours. In addition to their military training in which they never falter, they constantly remember the greatest and lofty name of Allah, and are preoccupied with worship day and night. This is why they always come out victorious".

❋

The Bayazit Mosque was opened for worship on a Friday and the first to lead the prayer there was the son of Fatih, Bayazid II himself. Evliya Chelebi explains this event as follows:

"After the mosque had been built, it was officially opened one Friday with great festivity. Bayazid II said to the congregation:

"Whoever has never abandoned the first *sunnah* prayer of the *asr* and *'isha* prayers, may he come forth and be the imam at this blessed time".

When no one in the congregation (which was like the ocean) rose, Bayazid Han had to rise:

"Praise be to Allah! We have never abandoned these *sunnah* prayers neither in war nor in peace..." and he became the imam and led the prayer".

❋

Safiye Hanim, or Muallima'i Selatin as she was otherwise known, was the Teacher of Sultans, appointed in order to raise and educate the children in the Ottoman Palace by Mehmed Rashad, the Sultan. One of the first commands to her by Mehmed Rashad was as follows:

"I will forbid salt and bread to those who do not pray and who do not fast. Let this wish of mine be declared to the student pashas and lady sultans by the lady teacher".[40]

Worldly rank and position did not allow these people to forget their sensitivity in worship nor did it prevent them from making efforts to make their provisions for the hereafter such as prayer and fasting, at the head of all of their duties.

❋

The most dynamic example of fastidiousness in worship is from the glorious *mujahid* of the Caucasus, Shaykh Shamil. He had suffered several bayonet, sword and bullet wounds during the Defence of Gimri in 1829. A bayonet that had entered through his

---

40. Safiye Unuvar, Saray Hatiralarim, Istanbul 1964, p 21).

breast and came out his back had pierced his lungs, and broken his ribs and his right collar bone. He was treated by his father-in-law who was also his surgeon, and it was only after a period of nearly 6 months that he was able to recover. This young *mujahid* had been in a coma for 25 days since the day he had been wounded. When he came to and opened his eyes at the end of the 25th day he found his mother at his side. His first words to her were:

"Dearest mother! Have I missed the time for prayer?

It was the eve of the Ramadan *eid* (festival) during the time when the Battle for the Dardanelles was being fought. The front commander, Wahip Pasha called the imam of the 9th battalion and said to him sadly and reluctantly:

"O Hafiz! Tomorrow is the *eid* of Ramadan. The soldiers wish to pray the *eid* prayer in congregation. No matter how I tried, I could not make them change their minds. But such a thing is very dangerous as it is an opportunity for the enemies to destroy us completely. Can you please try to explain the situation to the privates in a suitable way..."

The Imam had just left the Pasha's side when a radiant-looking individual appeared and said to him:

"My son! Make sure not to say anything to the soldiers! Let us wait and see what the day brings. Whatever Allah says will be".

The next morning a divine manifestation was experienced that left everyone in shock. Huge clouds hung down from the skies like bunches of fruit, covering the believing soldiers as they prayed in a state of love for Allah. The enemy soldiers who had been watching them with binoculars could see nothing but pure white clouds. That morning, the loud cries of *takbir* (Allahu Akbar) of the *eid* prayer ascended to the skies. Whilst the radiant old man read some verses from the chapter Victory from the Qur'an, the oneness of Allah overflowed from the hearts of the soldiers and could be heard from the enemy ranks.

It was at this point that chaos broke out amongst the British forces. The British had deceived various Muslim soldiers from their colonies and brought them to fight for them. When these Muslim soldiers heard the cries of *takbir* (Allah is the Greatest) and *tawheed* (La ilaha illallah) they realised that they were fighting Muslims like themselves and they subsequently rebelled. Not knowing what to do, the oppressive British executed some of them and others were hurriedly dragged to the back of the front.

Faith, the unwavering fortress in the hearts of the soldiers of Islam, enabled them to perform their worship even when on the battlefield and as a result divine success and help befell and enveloped the entire army.

❁

The Blessed Prophet ﷺ stated that the speed with which a person will pass over the bridge of Sirat will be in accordance to the degree to which they gave importance to their worship.

"People will come to the Fire and then will pass by according to their deeds: the first group will pass by at the speed of lightning, the second group like the wind. The next group will pass by as quick as horsemen and the next will pass by at the speed of a camel rider. The next one will run and the one after that will walk". (Tirmidhi, Tafsir, 19/3159).

❁

In short, the aim of worship and servanthood is that the heart should be together with Allah. That is, it should have knowledge of Allah (gnosis) and love for Him. Worship will bestow grace and beauty upon a person to the degree that faith has become apparent in their heart. Worship done with enthusiasm and ardour will bring depth to the soul and bring the servant closer to Allah. It will allow feelings of mercy and generosity to develop in their heart. Almighty Allah will become like the seeing eye and the hearing ear of such servants. That is to say, what they see, hear, think, and express will reach a state of divine illumination.

May our Lord make this possible for each of us. Amen!...

a. Supererogatory [optional] worship

Supererogatory worship reinforces the obligatory and is a means for the servant to approach Allah. As part of the nature of being human, it is not possible to perform obligatory worship completely and perfectly in a form that is the most acceptable to Allah. However much care may be taken, mistakes and faults will inevitably occur from time to time. Consequently there is no other remedy other than the supererogatory to make up for the deficiency. Allah's Messenger ﷺ has informed us that:

"On the day of judgement, the first deed that the servant will be taken to account for is the ritual prayer (salat). If the ritual prayer is complete, his affairs will be set aright and he will come out profitable. If his prayer is not complete he will lose and be deficient. If there is any deficiency in the obligatory worship, then the Lord Most Supreme and Glorious will say:

"Look and see whether my servant has any supererogatory prayers". The supererogatory will make up the deficiency in the obligatory. And then he will be taken to account in the same way for his other deeds". (Tirmidhi, Salat, 188/413).

However it should not be concluded that it is correct to leave the obligatory and occupy oneself with the supererogatory. Just as it is wrong to only busy oneself with the obligatory and neglect the supererogatory, it is also wrong to only perform the super-erogatory and neglect the obligatory. The correct way is to perform the obligatory and also make efforts to perform as much of the supererogatory as much as is possible. The practice of the Messenger of Allah and his Companions is the only guide in this matter.

On the other hand it is not right for those who have a debt in the obligatory to only make up for the obligatory and abandon the supererogatory all together. This is because one can make up for the obligatory prayers at any time of the day except for times which have been specifically identified as being reprehensible for worship. Whereas since all supererogatory prayers such as *tahajjud* (night prayers), *ishrak, kusluk (the late morning prayers), awabeen* (the late-evening prayer) are dependent on particular times, it is advisable to perform these prayers at these times[41].

The servant cannot approach Allah with any deed better than the obligatory. They can then continue this elevated journey by performing supererogatory worship. The Messenger of Allah ﷺ relates in a divine *hadith* that Allah has said:

"I wage war against the one who becomes an enemy of the friend of Mine who serves me in all sincerity. My servant draws nearer to Me with nothing more pleasing to Me than what I have made obligatory upon him, and then draws nearer to me with super-erogatory devotions until I love him and when I love him I become his hearing with which he hears, his sight with which he sees, his hand with which he strikes, and his foot with which he walks, so that by Me he hears, by Me he sees, by Me he strikes, and by Me he

---

41. The *mujtahid* scholars of the Hanafi School of thought are adamant that the *sunnah* prayers cannot be abandoned. It is only when at *sinn-i kebir*, that is old age, that is when one has lost the strength to carry out both the obligatory and the *sunnah* prayers that one can make up for their past obligatory instead of performing the *sunnah* prayers.

walks. Should he ask Me, I shall surely grant him his request; Should he ask Me for protection I shall surely protect him. Never do I hesitate in anything as I hesitate in taking the soul of my believing servant; he dislikes death, and I dislike to displease him". (Bukhari, Rikak, 38; Ahmad, VI, 256; Haysami, II, 248).

Supererogatory worship keeps the awareness of servanthood alive, and softens the heart. It refines the soul and bestows the light of gentle beauty upon the face. The excitement of faith of those who continue in their supererogatory worship with awe, contentedness and alertness of the heart, is greater and their desire for union is more exuberant. And of course their happiness and pleasure in the afterlife will manifest accordingly.

Scenes of Virtue

The days and nights of the Messenger of Allah ﷺ were enlightened by much continued supererogatory forms of worship in addition to the obligatory. The *sunnah* prayers that he prayed before and after the obligatory, the *tahajjud* prayer that he continued to pray in the night, worship such as rememberance and reflection, his recitation of a certain portion of the Qur'an every day, his different prayers such as the late morning and evening prayers, his supererogatory fasting, his giving charity to the poor, his struggles in the path of Allah, his continued smiles that blossomed like a rose on his blessed face were all signs of his peaceful togetherness with Allah. Whenever he was happy about something or when he received happy news he would prostrate[42] and pray[43]

---

42. The prostration of gratitude is like the prostration of recitation. While one has the ritual ablution, the intention is made to make the prostration of gratitude, the hands are raised and the takbir is pronounced, "*Allahu Akbar*", then a person prostrates and stays for as long as possible in that position, and then rises.
43. Ibn-i Majah Salat, 192

in order to thank Allah for this bounty. In the event of extraordinary events such as a solar or lunar eclipse he would immediately bow down in the face of such divine manifestations of magnificence[44]. When he had a need to ask for from Allah he would again perform the prayer. In the blessed month of Ramadan the Messenger of Allah became even more spiritual with the worship he performed such as the *tarawih* prayers, his *itikaf* (seclusion), and the generosity in giving out of the Messenger of Allah. After Ramadan he would continue to perform from time to time supererogatory fasting. He would especially choose to fast on Mondays and Thursdays and he would explain the reason as follows:

"*It is on Mondays and Thursdays that the deeds of a person are presented to Allah Most High. I like to have my deeds presented while I am fasting*". (Tirmidhi, Savm, 44/747).

On the 13th, 14th and 15th days of the *hijri* month called the '*days of white*' (due to the full moon) he would take care to fast and advised his Companions to do the same. Ibn-i Abbas states:

"The Prophet would fast on the days of the full moon in both war and peace and would never abandon this practice". (Nasai, Savm, 70)

Allah's Messenger would spend six days of the month of *Shawwal* fasting [45] and would fast the *Ashura* fast on the 9th and 10th or the 10-11th days of the month of Muharrem[46].

The Prophet would explain the virtues of the Greater and Lesser Pilgrimages (Hajj and Umrah) and he would be in a state of constant remembrance, and would never cease his praise, glorification and asking for forgiveness. He would sacrifice an animal

---

44. Bukhari, Kusuf, 2-4; Ibni Hibban, Sahih, Beirut, 1993, VII, 8, 100
45. Muslim, Siyam, 204
46. Muslim, Siyam 115

for himself and for those in his community who could not afford to. [47]

❋

Rabia bin Ka'b ﷺ narrates:

"I used to prepare the Messenger's ﷺ water for ablution and bring the things he needed to his door at nights. For a while I would hear him say 'Sami Allahu liman hamida' and then I would hear him say 'Alhamdulillahi Rabb al alemin'. (Ibn-i Sa'd, IV, 313).

One day The Messenger of Allah said to me:

"Ask me for whatever you want". I said:

"I want to be together with you in Paradise". The Prophet replied:

"Can't you ask for something else"? I said:

"This is the only thing I want" I said. Hearing this Allah's Messenger said:

"In that case, make much prostration so that you can help me help you". (Muslim, Salat, 226).

What is meant by prostration is generally the ritual prayer or salat. In that case those who want to enter Paradise and be a neighbour of the Beloved of Allah should pray much and increase their prostrations which are moments of closeness with Allah.

The station of the Prophet Muhammad ﷺ in Paradise is greater than that of all the other prophets. So if one desires to be close to the Prophet in Paradise, one should act in accordance with the sunnah and in particular, perform much ritual prayer (salat) in deep reverence.

❋

---

47. Abu Dawud, Edahi, 3-4/2792: Ibn-i Sa'd, I, 249

Ummu Habiba 🌸 narrates:

"The Messenger of Allah 🌸 said:

"*Allah will most certainly build a house in Paradise for whoever prays 12 cycles of supererogatory prayers in addition to the obligatory*". After hearing this good news from the Messenger of Allah I never abandoned any of these prayers". (Muslim, Musafirin, 103).

❋

On the day that Khaybar was conquered a man came to the Prophet and said:

"O Messenger of Allah, today I have made such a profit the likes of which none of the people of this valley have seen" The Prophet aksed him:

"*What did you earn?*" The Companion replied:

"I continued to buy and sell without stopping so much so that I earned 300 *ukiyye*[48]".

In response to this the Prophet 🌸 said:

"*Shall I tell you something that is the best of profits?*"

The Companion replied:

"What is that o Messenger of Allah?" The Prophet gave the following response:

"*Two cycles of supererogatory prayer that you pray after the obligatory prayer*". (Abu Dawud, 168/2785).

❋

Allah's Messenger 🌸 once sent a military troop to a certain region. In a very short period of time the soldiers of Islam returned with large amounts of booty. One individual said:

---

48. Ukiyye – an old measure of weight corresponding to 1283 grams.

"O Messenger of Allah! We have never seen a troop return as quickly as these and with as much booty".

The Messenger of Allah ﷺ asked:

"Shall I tell you something that has a faster return and brings more booty?" and then continued:

"If a man takes his ablution properly and then arrives at the mosque, and prays his dawn prayer and follows it up with two cycles of the midmorning prayer, then this man will have made a much faster return and will have gained much more". (Ibn-i Hibban, VI, 276/2535).

❋

Ibn-i Omar ﷺ narrates:

I said to Abu Dharr ﷺ:

"Dear uncle, can you give me some advice? He replied:

"You asked from me what I asked for from the Messenger of Allah. Allah's Messenger said to me:

"If you pray two cycles of the late-morning prayer you will not be written as amongst the ignorant; if you pray 4 cycles you will be written as a worshipper; if you pray 6 cycles, Allah will meet all of your needs; if you pray 8 cycles you will be recorded as a 'qanitin' (one who does much worship); if you perchance pray 10 cycles, a house will be built for you in Paradise".

There is no day, nor no night, and no second even in which Allah Most High does not bestow upon his servants what they wish and favours them. Allah Most High has not bestowed a bounty upon any of his slaves greater than the inspiration of His remembrance in his heart". (Haysami, II, 236; Ali al-Muttaki, VII, 809/21511).

❋

The Blessed Prophet ﷺ said:

"There is a door to Paradise which is called the Gate of Duha. On the Day of Judgement a Crier will cry out:

"Where are those who were continual in their Duha prayer? Here is your door, so enter into Paradise through it by the Mercy of Allah". (Suyuti, I, 355/2323).

❁

To pray at least two cycles of the ritual prayer after every minor and major ablution, and to thank almighty Allah for the bounty of Islam and the joy of carrying out ablution is a beautiful virtue.

As Othman ﷺ once said after he had taken his ablution in order to teach people:

"I saw the Messenger of Allah ﷺ take his ablution like this. And then when he had finished he said:

"Whoever takes ablution like I just did and performs two cycles of prayer and stays away from the whisperings of the nafs during the prayer, will have their past sins forgiven". (Bukhari, Wudu, 24)

❁

One time the Messenger of Allah ﷺ said to Bilal ﷺ:

"O Bilal! Which of your worship is it that you performed after you became Muslim that you hope for the most reward from? Because I heard the sounds of your shoes ahead of me in paradise". Bilal replied:

"After I have taken my ablution I pray as much prayer as I can, day and night. This is the worship that I hope for the most reward from". (Bukhari, Tahajjud 17, Tawheed 47, FAdailus – Sahaba 108).

Allah's Messenger saw Bilal in his dream walking ahead of him in Paradise. Almighty Allah showed the Prophet this dream to inform us of the importance of supererogatory prayers.

❋

One day Abu Qatada came to the Mosque of the Prophet. When he saw the Blessed Prophet sitting amongst his Companions he went and sat next to him. Upon this Allah's Messenger turned to Abu Qatada and said:

"*What prevented you from praying two cycles of prayer before you sat down?*" Abu Qatade replied:

"O Messenger of Allah! I saw that you and your congregation were sitting (so I did not pray)". The Prophet then said:

"*Whenever one of you enters the mosque let him not sit until he has prayed two cycles of prayer*". (Muslim, Musafirin, 70)

❋

Whenever the Companions needed anything or whenever they were in distress they immediately prayed supererogatory prayers and sought refuge with Allah. One summer's day the gardener of Anas 🌸 came to him and complained that it had not rained and that the garden had withered. Anas asked for some water and took his ablution following which he performed the prayer. After he finished, he asked the gardener:

"Do you see anything in the sky?" The gardener replied:

"No I do not".

Anas 🌸 went back inside and continued to pray. He asked again for the third or the fourth time:

"Can you see anything in the sky?" The gardener answered:

"I can see a cloud the size of a bird's wing". Upon this Anas continued his prayer and supplication. A little while later the gardener went next to him and said:

"The sky is full of clouds and it has started to rain". Anas said:

"Come, mount the horse that Bishr bin Shagaf sent and look and see how far the rain has reached".

When the gardener mounted the horse and looked around he saw that the rain had not reached beyond Anas's garden. (Ibn-i Sa'd, VII, 21-22).

The sensitivity of the blessed Companions for their supererogatory worship was also passed onto their children. Rubayyi' bint-i Muawwiz 🌸, who was one of the female companions says:

"... We used to fast on the day of *Ashura*. And we used to make our small children fast too. We would go to the mosque and makes toys out of wool for our children. Whenever one of them would cry for food we would hand him one of these toys and thereby distract them until the time came to break the fast". (Bukhari, Sawm, 47; Muslim, Siyam, 136).

In short, worship that has been specified as obligatory and commanded to do is the bare minimum. In addition to this minimum, the believers need to continue on in and increase their supererogatory worship. This they should do to the best of their ability, both out of a desire to be close to their Lord, and as gratitude for all the bounties that have reached them in times of ease or distress. Because the meaning of worship is to appear before Allah Most High and converse with Him. This is a peerless standing that submerges the hearts in mystic pleasure and allows them to enter a spiritual atmosphere.

The experience obtained from supererogatory worship and the efforts shown to this end, all eventually lead the servant to the stage of '*ihsan*', in which the servant is together with Allah always.

Supererogatory worship is the most fitting behaviour appropriate to the purpose of man's creation. It is also the servant's most vital provision for the hereafter.

b. Praying in Congregation

Social training is one of the most important principles of Islam. And the first lesson for the Muslim starts with praying in congregation. This is the most important deed that strengthens the feeling of unity and togetherness within the society of Islam, which is itself based on the oneness of Allah. A place in which the prayer is prayed in congregation is a place in which the spirit and societal structure of Islam has begun to be perceived.

Islam commands the believers to live within a community, to help and support each other in all matters, and to struggle as if they are one rank together and united in the path of Allah. Almighty Allah states:

"Allah loves those who fight in His Way in ranks like well-built walls". (As Saff, 61:4)

The Messenger of Allah ﷺ has said:

"...I desire that you be a community and that you avoid separation and division with an intensity. This is because Satan is with those who live on their own. But he stays far from people who live together even if they are only two (people). The person who wishes to be in the midst of Paradise should continue to pray in congregation..." (Tirmidhi, Fiten, 7/2165).

During each cycle of the prayer, we repeat the verse **"You alone do *we* worship and from You alone do *we* seek help".** (Fatiha, 1:4), thereby demonstrating to our Lord, at least 40 times a day, that we are part of a community.

The first thing that our Prophet did when he entered the cities of Quba and Madina was to build a mosque. He himself helped to build the mosque thereby laying the foundations of the brotherhood of Islam.

Our forefathers followed this practice of the Prophet. When they built cities they first of all built magnificent mosques at the centre and then developed the city around this mosque which acted as a circle of light.

Consequently to perform the prayer in congregation is most suited to the purpose of Islam and is a command of Allah.

The Prophet ﷺ has said:

"Allah Most High is as pleased and happy with the Muslim who frequents the mosque for both remembrance and prayer as a family who is away from home would be pleased when their relatives return". (Ibn-i Majah, Masajid, 19).

"Whoever befriends the mosque, Allah will befriend him". (Suyuti, II, 143).

"Shall I inform you how Allah Most High erases mistakes and how He raises one's station? Taking ablution on a cold day, going to a congregation from a far-off place, and waiting in anticipation of the next prayer having just prayed the previous one. This is true devotion! This is true devotion! This is true devotion!" (Muwatta, Kasru"s Salat, 55).

Aisha ﷺ states:

126

"Whoever hears the call for prayer and does not go to the mosque, means that he neither desires good nor has no good been willed for him". (Bayhaki, AS Sunan al Kubra, III, 57).

Allah's Messenger made no concessions for the one who was neglectful of praying in congregation. One day he said:

"Whoever hears the call to prayer and does not go to the mosque even though he has no excuse to prevent him, will not have his solitary prayer accepted (as a perfect prayer). The Blessed Companions asked him:

"(O Messenger of Allah) What is the excuse?"

The Prophet replied:

"The fear of danger or sickness". (Abu Dawud, Salat, 46/551).

To abandon praying in congregation will lead to the breaking up of the Islamic community. Almighty Allah condemns the one who splits the community as follows:

"As for those who divide up their religion and form into sects, you have nothing whatsoever to do with them". (An'am 6:159)

Scenes of Virtue

Abu Hurayra narrates:

"One time during an expedition, the Messenger of Allah stayed at a place between Dacnan and Usfan. The polytheists said:

"The Muslims have a prayer which is more precious to them than their own fathers and sons. This prayer is the afternoon prayer (*asr*). Prepare yourselves, and attack them all at once (while they are praying this prayer)".

127

Upon this the angel Gabriel came to the Messenger of Allah with the 102nd verse from Chapter *Nisa* which describes how to perform the congregational prayer during a battle. (Tirmidhi, Tafsir, 4/21).

Thus even during war, whatever the conditions, it was not even conceivable for the Muslims to delay their prayer or to abandon praying it in congregation.

Jafar bin Amr, narrates an anecdote he heard from his father:

"I saw the Messenger of Allah ﷺ cut off the forearm of a lamb and begin to eat it. At that point he was called to pray. He immediately rose, left the knife he was holding in his hand and without taking a fresh ablution, he stood to pray". (Bukhari, Adhan, 43)

Allah Messenger was so sensitive about praying in congregation that he immediately abandoned his food and rose to pray at the first calling, which could well have been delayed until after he had eaten.

❁

Yazid bin Amir ﷺ narrates:

"I arrived next to Allah's Messenger whilst he was praying. I sat down and did not join the congregation. When the Prophet turned around after the prayer he saw me sitting in the corner:

"O Yazid! Are you not a Muslim?"

"Indeed I am o Messenger of Allah". I said

"In that case what prevented you from joining in the congregation?" he asked.

"I thought that you would have already prayed the prayer so I prayed at home" I said. The Prophet then said:

*"If perchance you come to the prayer and you see people pray-
ing, join them. If you have already performed your prayer then this
will be accepted as supererogatory for you. The one you performed
at home will be considered as obligatory".* (Abu Dawud, Salat, 56/577).

❀

Even during the sickness of the Messenger of Allah ﷺ, which
was to be the cause of his death, one of the most important matters he was careful about was praying in congregation. According
to Anas ﷺ it was only during the last three days of his illness that
the Prophet was unable to join the congregation for prayer.
(Bukhari, Athan, 46).

Aisha ﷺ said:

"During the time when the Prophet was intensely sick he
asked:

"Have my Companions prayed?"

"No, o Messenger of Allah, they are waiting for you" I said

"In that case prepare some water for me" he said. I took him
some water and he washed himself. When he tried to get up he
fainted. He gained consciousness a little while later and asked once
more:

"Have my Companions prayed?"

"No, o Messenger of Allah, they are waiting for you" we said.

"In that, case prepare some water for me" he said. I brought
him some water and he washed. When he tried to get up he fainted. A little while later he regained consciousness.

This occurred again a few times. Meanwhile the people in the
mosque were waiting for the Prophet so they could pray the *'isha*
(nighttime) prayer. Then the Messenger of Allah sent word to Abu

Bakr for him to lead the prayer. Abu Bakr ☙ was a very tender-hearted man so he said to Omar ☙:

"O Omar, could you lead the prayer?" Omar could not accept his offer and responded:

"You are more worthy of this". Abu Bakr ☙ led the prayers during that time. Later on when the Messenger of Allah ☙ was feeling a little better he went to the mosque for the noon prayer, holding onto the arms of two men. (I can still see him in front of me, his blessed feet dragging along the floor because of his lack of strength when he walked)[49].

At that time, Abu Bakr ☙ was leading the prayer. When he saw that the Prophet had arrived he wanted to move back. However the Messenger of Allah ☙ signalled to him not to move from his spot. Then he came and sat next to Abu Bakr. Abu Bakr followed the Blessed Prophet, while the people followed Abu Bakr, and thereby completed their prayer (Bukhari, Athan, 51).

❀

Anas ☙ narrates:

"One time Abu Bakr was praying. It was a Monday and we were aligned in neat rows. The Messenger of Allah ☙ raised the curtain of his room and began to watch us. He was standing. His face was radiant. Then he smiled and his blessed teeth could be seen. When we saw the Blessed Prophet we were so happy that we were about to leave the prayer. Abu Bakr ☙ began to move back to enter the row behind him thinking that the Messenger of Allah would join the prayer. However the Prophet indicated to him to complete the prayer and closed his curtain. That was the last day that we saw him and the day he passed on to the world of eternity". (Bukhari, Athan, 46)

---

49. Bukhari, Athan, 67

The Messenger of Allah was delighted that he had left behind a community that stood in neat rows to pray, like a building strengthened with lead and which continued to pray in congregation. When he watched them, his blessed face was smiling. This smile that lit up the entire universe was a source of hope for the blessed Companions, (but they had to accept that) he had finally turned, with peace of mind, towards Allah and was waiting for the moment of reunion.

The last words of the Blessed Messenger ﷺ during his death were:

"*Your prayer! Your prayer! Be especially careful about your prayer. And fear Allah about what is under your control*". (Abu Dawud, Adab,m 123-4/ 5156; Ibn-i Majah, Wasaya, 1).

❁

Jabir bin Abdullah ﷺ narrates:

"The neighbourhood of my tribe, Bani Salim, was rather far from the mosque. There were some vacant sites around the Prophet's mosque so we wanted to sell our house and move closer to the mosque. At that time the following verse was revealed:

"We bring the dead to life and We record what they send ahead and what they leave behind. We have listed everything in a clear register". (Yasin 36:12)

When he heard of our intention, the Messenger of Allah ﷺ said to us:

"I hear that you wish to move closer to the mosque, is this true?" They said:

"Yes, o Messenger of Allah. We truly wish for this".

Then the blessed Prophet said:

131

"O Bani Salim! Remain where you are and receive a reward for each step you take in coming to the mosque. Yes, remain where you are; and let there be a reward written for every step you take in coming to the mosque". (Muslim, Masajid, 280, 281; Tirmidhi, Tafsiru'l Qur'an, 36/1).

❋

Abdullah bin Ummi Maktum ﷺ once asked the Prophet:

"O Messenger of Allah, the poisonous insects and wild animals of Madina are many. (I fear the harm that may come to me from these animals. Is there then a licence for me to stay in my home and pray rather than coming to the mosque?"

The Messenger of Allah ﷺ replied:

"Can you hear the words: "hayya ala's-salah" (come to the prayer) and "hayya ala'l falah" (come to success)? If so, you should come to the mosque". (Abu Dawud, Salat, 46/553).

Thus whatever the circumstances, the Prophet placed great importance on participation in the congregation even if one has to make a great effort.

The Messenger of Allah ﷺ used to warn people to come to the congregation in various ways. Ubayy bin Ka'b ﷺ narrates:

"One day the Messenger of Allah ﷺ led the dawn prayer and said:

"Did such and such come for the prayer?"

"No, he did not" we replied

"Did such and such come?" he asked

"No, he did not" we replied. Upon this he said:

"It is these two prayers (the dawn and the night time prayer) that are the hardest on the hypocrites. If you knew how much reward

and merit there was in these, you would get down on your knees and crawl to join the congregation. The first row is like a row of angels. If you knew the virtue within it, you would race each other to pray in that row. A person's prayer prayed together with another person is much more bountiful and has more reward than a prayer performed alone. A prayer with two people is more bountiful and superior than a prayer with one other person. However great the number of people praying, the more Allah Most High is pleased". (Abu Dawud, Salat, 47/554; Nasai, Imamet, 45)

❀

Abdullah bin Mas'ud ﷺ has the following to say:

"By Allah I have never seen a person, other than a hypocrite whose hypocrisy was known by all, who neglected his prayer. I swear by Allah that a (sick) man would be brought to the prayer even though he was teetering on two feet, held between two men and would be placed in the row amongst those two men as support". (Muslim, Masajid, 256-257)

❀

One day when Abdullah bin Omar ﷺ was walking in the marketplace, the time for prayer came. He saw the Muslims closing their shops and stalls as soon as they heard the call to prayer, and heading for the mosque. Seeing this he said:

"These are they who Allah Most High has praised in the following way:

"**There are men who proclaim His glory morning and evening, not distracted by trade or commerce from the remembrance of Allah and the establishment of salat and the payment of zakat; fearing a day when all hearts and eyes will be in turmoil**". (An Nur, 24:37) (Ibn-i Kathir, Tafsir, III, 306; Haysami, VII, 83).

❀

133

Shifa bint-i Abdillah 🌸 narrates:

"One day Omar bin Khattab 🌸 came to see us. When he saw two members of our family sleeping he asked:

"What is wrong with these men that they did not join me in the congregation?"

"O Commander of the Believers! They prayed together with everyone in the evening – this event took place during the month of Ramadhan – and they continued to pray until the morning. After that they prayed the dawn prayer and went to bed" I said. Omar responded as follows:

"To pray the dawn prayer in congregation is more pleasing to me than praying until morning". [50]

❈

One time Othman bin Affan 🌸 had gone to the night time prayer. When he saw that the congregation was sparse he lay down at the back of the mosque and waited for more people to arrive.

At that point Ibn-i Abi Amre 🌸 arrived and sat down next to Othman. Othman asked him who he was. He introduced himself. "How much do you know of the Qur'an? He asked. After replying to this Othman said:

"O son of my brother! I heard the Messenger of Allah 🌸 say:

"The one who prays the night time prayer with the people (in congregation) is like the one who has spent half the night in prayer. The one who prays the dawn prayer in congregation is like one who has spent the whole night in prayer". (Muwatta, Salatu'l Camaa' 7; Muslim, Masajid, 260)

❈

---

50. Abdurrazak, al Musannaf, Beirut 1970, I, 526; Muwatta, Salatu"l Jamaa, 7

Thabit bin Hajjaj narrates a hadith which reflects the attitude towards those who did not participate in the congregational (prayer):

"Omar bin Khattab 🙵 once came to the mosque for prayer. He turned towards the people, ordered the caller to prayer to read the call to prayer, and stood up saying:

"We will not wait for anyone to pray". After he had performed the prayer he turned to the congregation and said: "What is wrong with certain people that they refrain from praying in congregation and thereby make others refrain as well. By Allah it occurred to me to send some men to them to catch them and bring them here and warn them to join the prayer. (Abdurrazzak, 1, 519).

❊

Ummu-d Darda 🙵 narrates:

"Abu-d Darda 🙵 once came to me angrily. I asked him:

"What is it that has angered you?". He gave the following response:

"By Allah I know of nothing of the community of Muhammed 🙵 other than they're praying in congregation. (Why are these people behaving neglectfully towards the prayer?) (Bukhari, Athan, 31)

❊

Whenever Abdullah bin Omar 🙵 missed a congregational prayer he would occupy himself with worship until the next prayer. In fact this rule of his applied to the night time prayer as well. That is, in such a situation he would worship until the morning. (Ibn-i Hajar, Isabe, II, 349).

❊

Harith bin Hassan ﷺ one of the blessed Companions, was recently married. At that time it was the custom for a man who was newlywed to not leave the house for several days, so he did not go to the dawn prayer. However Harith attended the dawn prayer after the night he got married. He was asked by some:

"You were married last night, how can you have left your house already?" His response to them was:

"By Allah! How ruinous is a wife that would prevent me from praying the dawn prayer in congregation". (Haysami, II, 41).

Ibn-i Jurayj, once asked Ata' ﷺ who was from amongst the famous scholars from the *tabieen*:

"If someone is praying the obligatory prayer in his home and he hears (either of) the two calls to prayer, is he required to leave his prayer and go to the mosque?"

"If he is hopeful that he will be able to catch some part of the obligatory prayer, yes he is" Ata answered.

"What if I hear the second call to prayer, do I have to come to the mosque like I would if I heard the first call?" Ata answered 'yes' to this question. (Abdurrazzak, I, 514).

Likewise Ibn-i Omar (may Allah be pleased with) had once prayed two of the four cycles of an obligatory prayer in his home when he heard the second call to prayer and so he immediately went to the mosque (Abdurrazzak, I, 514-515).

Amir bin Abdullah was on his death bed. His breaths were numbered and those around him were crying. When he heard the evening call to prayer he said to those around him:

"Lift me up".

"What's the matter, where to?" they asked.

"To the mosque" he said. Those around him asked in surprise:

"In this state?"

With great fortitude, he said:

"Subhanallah! (Glory be to Allah!). Should I hear the call to prayer and not answer the call? Is this possible? Lift me up!"

"He went to the mosque accompanied by those close to him and after praying one cycle with the imam, he passed away while he was in prostration".

What a beautiful manifestation of the *hadith*, *"However you live that is how you shall die?"* By the grace of almighty Allah, a servant who had placed so much importance throughout his life on praying in congregation took his last breath while in prostration.

❋

Ata bin Thabit narrates:

"We heard that one of the friends of Allah, Abdullah-i Sulami was sick. We thought that we should go and visit him. They told us that he was staying at the mosque. We thought this a little strange. For him to live in the mosque when he had a bed at home appeared a little strange to us. When we went to the mosque we found him praying. When we saw that he was having trouble breathing we were afraid and said:

"O Shaykh! Would not you be more comfortable if you were home in bed?"

He gave the following reply:

"According to a *hadith* that reached me, the Messenger of Allah ﷺ informed us that praying in congregation is better. I would wish that my soul be taken while I am praying at the mosque".

Muhammad bin Sammad was a very worshipful individual. He was very sensitive when it came to the issue of praying in congregation. He says:

"I perform my prayers in congregation. For forty years I have never once missed the opening *takbir* of the prayer. Only once when I was busy with my mother's funeral did I fail to reach the first cycle of a prayer. I performed this prayer 25 times in the hope that I would get the reward of the congregational prayer. That night in my dream it was said to me:

"O Muhammad! You have prayed your prayer 25 times, however how are you going to make up for the angels saying amen in the congregational prayer?" (Kandevli, Fazail'i A'mal, pg 275).

The Messenger of Allah ﷺ once said:

"*When the imam finishes reading the Fatiha let the congregation say 'amen'. Because if this word of the congregation coincides with the 'amen' of those in the heavens, then the entirety of that person's past minor sins will be forgiven*". (Bukhari, Athan, 113).

According to the narrations, on the Day of Judgement Allah Most High will ask:

"Where are my neighbours?

The angels will ask:

"Who could be a neighbour to you o Lord?"

Allah Most High will say:

"Those who render my mosques prosperous (that is those who continue to pray in congregation)". (Ali al Muttaki, VII, 578/20339).

Allah's Messenger 🕮 states:

"The mosque is the home of all of those who are pious. Allah Most High has promised those who make their homes mosques, comfort, mercy and passing over the Bridge of Sirat and into paradise, and gaining Allah's pleasure" [51]

✿

One of the first Ottoman historians, Asik Pashazade, once said:

"This family of Othman comes from a noble lineage. There has never appeared from them an unlawful act. They avoided with their utmost all behaviour and deeds which the scholars deemed to be sinful"

Their above-mentioned behaviour must be the reason that the Shaykhu'l Islam, Molla Fenari, had the courage to refuse the witnessing of Yildirm Bayazit in court because he did not (pray) in congregation. In reply to the Sultan who asked him the reason he said quite openly:

"My Sultan! I do not see you in the congregation. Whereas, since you are the guide of this nation, you should be in the first row. In other words, you should be a person of righteous deeds... If you do not join the congregation you will be a bad example for your people, which will prevent you from being accepted as a witness..."

---

51. Taberani, Al Mu'jemu'l abir, tah. Hamdi Abdulmecid as Salafi, Beirut, Daru Ihyai't turasi'l Arabi, VI, 254/6143; Ali al Muttaki, VII, 580/20349

After this event, and in another report as gratitude for the victory at Nigbolu, Yildirim Bayazid had the famous Ulu Mosque of Bursa built and prayed there in congregation five times a day.

❀

In short, praying in congregation is a manifestation of the fidelity of one's faith. Likewise the Prophet ﷺ said:

"If you see a person regularly praying at the mosque then you can be a witness for his faith" and then he read the following verse:

"The mosques of Allah should only be frequented by those who have faith in Allah and the Last Day and establish salat and pay zakat, and fear no one but Allah. They are the ones most likely to be guided" (Tawba, 9:18)(Tirmidhi, Iman, 8/2617)

The friends of Allah have stated the principal benefits of praying in congregation at the mosque five times a day:

- Benefitting from the prosperity and bounty that Allah bestowed upon the mosques and the strengthening of social consciousness in the heart of the believer;

- Performing the prayer at the most acceptable of times, that is, at the first instant;

- Being subject to the supplication, seeking forgiveness for and witnessing of the angels;

- Being distant from Satan;

- Attaining to a great reward by being present for the opening *takbir*;

- Becoming purified of ostentation in one's deeds;

- Benefiting from the supplication and remembrance done in community;

- Ensuring the continuity of relations amongst the Muslims;

- Helping each other in matters of obedience and worship;

- Becoming acquainted with and learning the rules of recitation (of the Qur'an) in the prayers that are read out loud;

- Performing the prayer with perfection and in a peaceful manner;

As can be seen praying in congregation has many benefits. This is the reason that Allah Most High and His Beloved Prophet persistently ordered the believers to pray in the mosques and to continue praying in congregation.

c. Night Worship

It is an indescribable source of pleasure for the servant to be together with Almighty Allah in the depths of the night. It is also a means to unparalleled mercy, forgiveness and grace because Allah is pleased and content with such deeds. The Holy Qur'an states:

"Their sides eschew their beds as they call on their Lord in fear and ardent hope. And they give of what We have provided for them" (As Sajda, 32:16)

The mysteries, wisdom and prosperity that our Lord has bestowed upon the night become apparent according to the state of one's heart. Such divine favours as the Ascension and revelation, and also manifestations of divine revenge, have all taken place more often during the depths of night which is an indication that one should take extra care at this time of day.

For the believers who have aspired to draw nearer to Allah, the night is a peerless blessing due to the serenity and prosperity of the stillness of night time. It has been stated in a *hadith*:

"There is a certain time in the night in which if the Muslim makes a wish for good in this world or the next at this hour, then Allah grants it. This time occurs every night" (Muslim, Musafirin, 166).

Khaja Ali Ramiteni has said:

"It is when three hearts unite that the desire of the believer is granted; the sincere heart of the believer, the heart of the Qur'an which is chapter Yasin, and the heart of night which is the time just before dawn. Those who appreciate the value of this blessing find a most prosperous grounds for supplication, worship and turning towards their Sustainer, when all of creation has laid down to rest and there is a deep stillness throughout the world. Almighty Allah praises those happy slaves as follows:

"The part of the night they spent asleep was small and they would seek forgiveness before the dawn". (Az Zariyat 51:17-18)

The night is the time to abandon the soft and sweet beds for the sole purpose of gaining Allah's good pleasure. It is the time to enter the divine presence solely out of love and ecstasy. Consequently the prayers that are performed during the peaceful atmosphere of the night, and the Qur'an that is recited and the glorification that is performed have great importance in terms of approaching Allah. Worship that is carried out during the night is like meeting with an Exalted Lover and conversing with Him. Staying awake while everyone else is asleep, and entering the merciful atmosphere of Allah, the Most Dignified Protector, is to be included amongst the exceptional slaves who form an assembly of love and mercy.

The rush to do night worship is relative to the intensity of rapture and love of Allah felt in the heart. Certain worshippers who have tasted the spiritual pleasure and delight of night time worship have said: "I do not fear death, until it comes between me and my night prayers".

How can someone who claims to love their Lord in truth, sleep in deep heedlessness until the morning? This is why to bring life to the pre-dawn is an expression of the sincere love and reverence felt by the slave for his Lord. On the other hand a night passed in heedlessness or one confined to sleep is considered fruitless and an irreparable loss, just like the rain that falls in the desert.

Thus the Messenger of Allah ﷺ advised Abdullah bin Amr bin As ﷺ as follows:

"Abdullah! Do not be like such and such. Because though he used to continue in his night worship, he has now abandoned it" (Bukhari, Tahajjud, 19).

Thus it is a great loss and source of harm to refrain from doing *tahajjud* in the night.

Benefitting from the night begins with "seeking forgiveness"; and continues with surrounding oneself in the spiritual atmosphere of *tawheed*, sending blessings upon the Prophet (*salawat-i sherif*) and remembering Allah. Remembrance during the pre-dawn, which is like the meeting of the slave with his Protector is, in regards to bringing the heart back to life, a singular opportunity not to be missed, and a need which cannot be overlooked. For just as our bodies have need for physical nourishment so too does our soul need spiritual sustenance. Almighty Allah places more value on the remembrance done during the pre-dawn than at any other time. It is stated in the Qur'an:

"Prostrate to Him during the night and glorify Him throughout the long night. These people love this fleeting world and have put the thought of a Momentous Day behind their backs". (Man, 76:26-27)

Amr bin Abasa ﷺ narrates:

143

I asked the Messenger of Allah:

"O Messenger of Allah! Is there a time out of all times that is more virtuous than others in terms of drawing nearer to Allah?"

He answered:

"Yes, the time at which the slave is nearest to his Lord is the middle of the last part of the night. If you have the capacity to be of those people who remember Allah at that time, then do so. Because the prayer at that time is witnessed (the angels are present during them)". (Nesai, Mawakit"s Salat, 35).

In short, if the believer can make use of the night purposefully, in the way advised by Allah and His Messenger, and benefit from the spirituality of remembrance, then his night can be brighter than his day. Likewise Bayazid-i Bistami has said:

"No mystery has been revealed to me until my nights have become like my day".

For those who know the value of the night which is full of great bounty and thus bring it to life in the proper manner, the spirituality of the pre-dawn will reflect throughout their whole day. In respect to this, in order to properly benefit from the atmosphere of spirituality and prosperity of the night we need to project the model of the pre-dawn to our days and guard our days from sin.

Scenes of Virtue

In terms of benefitting from the prosperous atmosphere of the night, Almighty Allah commands His Beloved as follows:

"And stay awake for prayer during part of the night as a supererogatory action for yourself. It may well be that your Lord will raise you to a Praiseworthy Station". (Isra, 17: 79)

After this divine command was revealed the Messenger of Allah ﷺ never abandoned praying during the blessed and fruitful night, nor did he stop seeking forgiveness, reading the Qur'an and supplicating. He did this even during his times of sickness when he was weak and could not even stand on his feet. He did not neglect his *tahajjud* prayer and brought life to his nights even if sitting. (Abu Dawud, Tatavvu", 18/1307).

The Blessed Prophet continued to pray his *tahajjud* prayer throughout his whole life. This was a total of 13 cycles, if the *witr* prayer is included, and 11 cycles during the final years of his life. He continued to pray 9 cycles of the prayer while he was sick and close to death. (Abu Dawud, Tatawwu' 26/1363).

❋

The Prophet's wife, Aisha ﷺ has informed us:

"The Messenger of Allah ﷺ never prayed more than 11 cycles of prayer in the night, neither in Ramadan nor at any other time. First he would pray four cycles which were indescribable in terms of beauty and length. Then he would pray four more. Don't ask about their beauty and length (for they are hard to describe). Then he would pray three more. One time I asked him:

"O Messenger of Allah! Are you going to sleep without praying the *witr* prayer?"

"Aisha! My eyes sleep but my heart never sleeps," he replied. (Bukhari, Tahajjud 16, Tarawih 1; Muslim, Musafirin 125).

This *hadith* is an indication of how the heart of the Prophet was with Almighty Allah, not just during worship but at all times.

❋

Huzayfa ﷺ describes the state of the Prophet during worship one time when he was following the Prophet in a supererogatory prayer:

"One night I stood to pray with the Messenger of Allah. He began to read chapter *Baqara* from the Qur'an. *"He will probably bow down when he comes to the one hundredth verse"* I said to myself. When he came to the one hundredth verse he continued reading. *"Maybe he is going to pray two cycles with this chapter"* I thought to myself. He continued reading. *"He will bow down when he finishes the chapter"* I thought. However he still did not finish. He began to read from chapter *Nisa*. When he finished that he moved onto chapter *Al-i Imran*[52]. He was reading very slowly. When he came to a verse of glorification he would say "*Subhanallah* (Glory be to Allah). When he came to a verse about supplication, he would supplicate. When he came to a verse about seeking refuge in Allah, he would seek refuge in Allah. Then he bowed down. He began to say *"Subhana Rabbiya'l a'zim"* (Glory be to my Lord, Most Great) His bowing down lasted as long as his standing. Then he said *"Sami Allahu liman hamida. Rabbena laka'l hamd"* (Allah hears all praise. All praise is for you our Lord) and straightened up. He stayed standing for almost as long as he stood bowing down. Then he went into prostration. He said *"Subhana Rabbiya'l ala"* (Glory be to my Lord, most High). His prostration lasted almost as long as his standing" (Muslim, Musafirin, 203).

❈

Aisha ﷺ has said:

---

52. According to the explanation of this hadith, the Prophet ﷺ read first Baqara, then Nisa, then Al'i Imran. The reading of these in this order is not the same as the present order of the chapters in the Qur'an, which is Baqara, Al'i Imran, Nisa. (Commentators) of hadith explain the wisdom behind this in two ways: Firstly, the order of the chapters had not yet been determined at that time. Secondly, it is permissible to read the chapters in this order.

"One night I realised that the Messenger of Allah was not beside me. I thought that he might have gone to one of his other wives. I began to look for him. After a while when I came back, I saw him either bowing down or in prostration saying the following:

$$\text{سُبْحَانَكَ وَبِحَمْدِكَ لَا إِلَه إِلاَّ أَنْتَ}$$

"(O Allah!) I absolve You of all faults and I praise You. (My Sustainer! There is no god but You)". Upon this I said to him, (a little embarrassingly):

"May my mother and father be sacrificed for you o Messenger of Allah! What have I been busying myself with and what have you..." (Muslim, Salat, 221).

❊

The Messenger of Allah ﷺ desired that his entire community perform the *tahajjud* prayer, which is one of the most important means of spiritual growth. He began to instill this practice firstly into those close to him. One night he knocked on the door of his son-in-law and daughter, Ali ﷺ and Fatima ﷺ and said: *"Are you not going to perform the prayer?"* He was persistent in his advice to them to benefit from the spiritual prosperity of the night.

To others of his Companions he said:

"Make efforts to wake up in the night. For that was the practice of those righteous people before you and it is a means of approaching Allah. (This form of worship) will stop you from sinning, is an atonement for your mistakes, and will remove the worries from the body" (Tirmidhi, Deawat, 101/3549). Stating so, he invited them to remain awake during the pre-dawn.

❊

The mother of Solomon ﷺ, the son of the Prophet David, said to her son Solomon:

"My dear child! Do not sleep much during the night. For too much sleep during the night will render a person poor on the Day of Judgement" (Ibn-i Majah, Ikamet'us Salah, 174).

❈

The following event related by Ibn-i Omar ﷺ evidently explains how the *tahajjud* prayer will keep a person far from the punishment of the hellfire:

"Whenever anyone had a dream during the lifetime of the Prophet, they would tell him about it. I dearly wished to have a dream and tell the Prophet about it.

At that time I was a single young man and I used to sleep in the mosque.

One time during one of my dreams, two angels came and took me to Hell. I saw that there were two columns built like the walls of a well. I was surprised as there were some people that I knew there. I began to scream:

"I seek refuge in Allah from the fire of hell. I seek refuge in Allah from the fire of hell". At that time another angel came and said to me:

"Fear not, nothing will happen to you"

I shared this dream with my older sister Hafsa ﷺ and she related it to the Messenger of Allah ﷺ. Upon this the Prophet said: *"How beautiful and good a man is Abdullah! If only he prayed during the night as well..."*

From that day on, Abdullah ﷺ spent a large portion of the night in worship and slept very little. (Bukhari, Ashabu'n Nabi, 19).

❈

The Messenger of Allah ﷺ, in a divine *hadith*, has praised those believers who secretly give out, who wake up for *tahajjud* prayer and who strive earnestly in the way of Allah as follows:

"There are three types of people whom Allah loves. And there are three types of people who Allah detests. When it comes to the people that Allah loves:

A man approaches a group of people and asks them for something, not out of any familiarity to them but merely for the sake of Allah. They do not give him what he wants. One person from this congregation slowly moves to the back, without anyone realising and secretly gives this person what he wants. (He does it so secretly) that only Allah and the person he has helped know.

(When it comes to the second person): a group of travellers have been walking all night. They become so tired that sleep becomes dearer to them than anything else. They stop somewhere for the night. (All of them sleep). Only one of them gets up and supplicates to Me with humility and recites my verses.

(The third one is as such:) a person has joined a military expedition. They face the enemy but meet with a crushing defeat. Only this person moves on and continues to fight until he is killed or made victorious.

The three types of people that Allah detests are the old person who commits fornication, the poor man who is arrogant, and the rich man who is an oppressor" (Tirmidhi, Jannah, 25/2568; Nasai, Zakat, 75).

According to a report by Ali ﷺ, the Messenger of Allah ﷺ said:

"There are certain types of palaces in Paradise. The outside can be seen from the inside and the inside can be seen from the outside". Hearing this, a Bedouin stood up and asked:

"Who are these palaces for o Messenger of Allah?" The Prophet replied:

"For the one who speaks his words sweetly and nicely, who is soft-spoken, who likes to feed others, who continues to fast and who performs the prayer for the sake of Allah while everybody is sleeping" (Tirmidhi, Birr, 53/1984).

Our most honoured teacher Master Musa has informed us of the character of the eminent guide Mahmud Sami Ramazanoglu. He speaks of his elevated character in the way of gnosis of Allah (knowledge of Allah) and servanthood and his state in bringing life to his nights as follows:

"Though the noble face and blessed countenance of Mahmud Sami Ramazanoglu was always smiling, his heart would be inwardly weeping. He would shed tears for the community of Muslims and pray that they be freed from the hands of oppressors. He would cry for sinners to be saved and forgiven and his tears would flow inside. When the Qur'an was recited, he would listen in awe, and sometimes his tears would trickle down his cheeks. During the time of the Pilgrimage while he was moving between Madina and Mecca, his tears could be seen dripping down like pearls from his eyes, while his companions were sleeping, under the light of the moon,. This scene was of such beauty that even poets and literaries found it difficult to describe"

The fervour for night worship of the late Musa Topbas, can be compared to the indescribable longing and desire a lover feels in anticipation of the meeting with his beloved. This state of his continued even during his days of illness when his body was suffering and ailing such that he lived at a continual peak of divine love. After an eye operation and when he had just woken up from the effects of the anaesthetic the first question he asked those around him was:

"What time is it?"

When it was said to him

"Master! It is almost 3", he said:

"Night worship is most crucial" and with the help of those around him he took his dry ablution (*tayammum*) and as if forgetting the painful state he was in, he offered his heart to his Sustainer and prayed two cycles of *tahajjud* prayer (by moving his eyes). He did this with indescribable pleasure and enthusiasm, and then he began to perform his regular remembrance of Allah and glorification. This state of his was like an explanation of the mystery of the following verse:

"Their sides eschew their beds as they call on their Lord in fear and ardent hope. And they give of what We have provided for them" (As Sajda, 32:16)

✤

One day it was said to Ibrahim bin Edham:

"I cannot wake up for night worship, teach me a remedy for this"

He received the following reply:

"Do not rebel against Allah during the day and He will allow you into His presence during the night. To be in His presence during the night is the most elevated honour. Sinners are not worthy of this honour!"

✤

Night worship is the most important means to attaining both spiritual and bodily health.[53] Night worship repels sickness, and bestows physical and spiritual strength, sagacity and majesty. How cautionary is the following event:

During the Battle of Yarmak when the two armies had approached each other, the Greek commander sent an Arab spy to determine the state of the Muslim soldiers. After the spy had carried out the necessary intelligence he was asked on his return:

"What is the state of the Muslims? What are they doing? The spy told them of what he had seen as follows:

بِاللَّيْلِ رُهْبَانٌ وَبِالنَّهَارِ فُرْسَانٌ

"They are a nation worshipful by night and cavalrymen by day"

Upon this the commander gave the following response:

"If what you say is true, then to be under the earth (that is, dead) would be better than fighting them above ground"

The following event is similar:

No enemy was able to overpower the Companions of Allah's Messenger during battle. Heracles, the Greek commander of the army that was defeated, said to his army in anger:

"Shame on you! Are the people you are fighting not human beings like yourselves?"

"Indeed they are", they answered.

"Well are you greater in number, or are they?" he asked

---

53. See Tirmidhi, Deavat, 101/3549

"Sir, we are much greater than them in all respects" they answered.

"So what is wrong with you that every time you face them you meet with crushing defeat?" Upon this a wise, old man from amongst the Greek old men stood up and made the following analysis:

"They pass their nights in worship, they fast during the day, they keep their promise, they command to good and they shun evil, and they share everything amongst themselves...(and this is why we cannot defeat them)"

Upon this Heracles said:

"You have spoken the truth" [54]

In conclusion, the night is a unique time for keeping the mind and heart clear; the perception, emotions and expression sharp; and the memory strong. It is a fast and easy way to advance both physically and spiritually. The night time is an opportunity not to be missed for those who wish to prepare for the great duties that await them during the day. It is a time to brew the character of those pious, committed and conscious people, who struggle for the reformation of society. The true mysteries of the peace-filled night can only be revealed to those righteous believers who are able to bring life to their nights by intensifying their worship and reflection. The hearts of those slaves who possess these mysteries and wisdom can extend as wide as the heavens and earth and become mirrors for divine manifestation, enveloping themselves in knowledge of Allah.

O our Sustainer! Save us from wasting our nights in igno-rance and loss in this short fleeting life of ours. Bestow upon us

---

54. Ibn-i Asakir, Tarihu Dimask, ts., II, 97)

some of the mysteries of the night! Rejuvenate our hearts with the showers of prosperity that fall during the nights which are brought to life. Allow us to attain to the morning of the hereafter from this world which is like one short night, as true lovers having obtained Your Pleasure and let our souls taste the pleasure of union with You... Amen!

d. Prayer and Supplication

When the slave comes face to face with Allah's greatness and majesty, he must admit to his own weakness. He then seeks His help and bounty amongst feelings of devotion and reverence. This is prayer and supplication.

Supplication, that is, seeking refuge through prayer, is of great importance in religion as it is an expression of one's helplessness and a sign of one's taking refuge at nowhere else but the Divine court.

The slave should perform his supplication to Almighty Allah, not merely with words, but wholeheartedly and in all sincerity. Prayers should be said in a spiritual state of being between '*khawf* and *reja*' that is, 'fear and hope'. Prayer must come from the heart; the heart must tremble with a desire that is consistent with the meaning of the words of the prayer. If one is asking to be forgiven for a certain sin, then there should be decisiveness and absolute determination in this prayer. Jalaluddin al Rumi has said:

"Supplicate and seek forgiveness with teary eyes and a heart burning full of regret. For flowers bloom where there is heat and moisture".

Under all circumstances and as a requirement of being a slave, the believer should be in a state of entreaty to his Lord. The aim of true religious training is for the spirit of the believer to be in a continual state of supplication. This is because prayer is the key to the highest door of the heart that leads one to Allah. The Holy Qur'an states:

"If My slaves ask you about Me, I am near. I answer the call of the caller when he calls on Me" (Baqara, 2:186)

As prayer is repeated it becomes engraved onto the spirit of the believer with profound and meaningful feelings, penetrating his personality until they become a part of his character. It is for this reason that great and elevated spirits live in a continual state of supplication.

Supplication is when we turn to Almighty Allah, who is the Possessor of eternal power, with true perception of our helplessness and bow our heads down in His presence in submission and a state of serenity. To begin our supplication admitting our helplessness and our faults is to invite Divine Compassion and thus has great influence on the acceptance of our prayer.

The Prophet ﷺ taught us how to pray in the best way. In addition to his *salat* which he performed in tears and until his ankles swelled up, he also sought refuge in Almighty Allah all the time with feelings of helplessness. He loved concise prayers and did not utter prayers that were not concise.[55] He used to advise the following:

"The point at which the slave is closest to his Lord is in prostration. For this reason you should look to making much supplication while in prostration". (Muslim, Salat, 215)

Aside from praying consistently, the believer should also make efforts to gain the prayers of his brother in religion, and the poor, weak and needy. Because our Prophet ﷺ said:

---

55. Abu Dawud, Vitir, 23/1482)

"There is no prayer that is accepted faster than the prayer a Muslim makes for another Muslim in his absence" (Tirmidhi, Birr, 50/1980).

Jalaluddin Al Rumi has the following to say:

"Look to giving out from yourself, your wealth, and your property in order to please hearts. So let the prayer of that heart be light and illumination for you, while you are in the pitch blackness of the grave...."

Scenes of Virtue

One day the Messenger of Allah ﷺ said:

"If a Muslim asks for something from Allah, Allah Most High will definitely grant his wish or He will remove evil from him in proportion to what He would have given him, as long as he does not ask for anything sinful or does not cut his relations with his relatives"

One of his Companions said:

"In that case we desire many things from Allah". The Messenger of Allah responded as such:

"Allah's grace is greater than the things you ask from Him" (Tirmidhi, Deavat, 115/3573; Ahmad, II, 18).

Almighty Allah does not reject sincere prayers. However He does not accept certain demands made that do not comply with Absolute Destiny, even though they may be asked for in complete sincerity. However, the slave should never give up and should continue to pray. This is because in those cases the response to the prayer has been deferred to the afterlife. Almighty Allah has said:

"Your Lord says, "Call on Me and I will answer you" (Mu'min, 23:60)

The Prophet Muhammad ﷺ said:

"The prayer of the slave will be answered as long as he does not ask for something that will lead to sin or to his relations with his relatives being severed and if he is not impatient about the result"

He was asked:

"O Messenger of Allah! What does it mean for him to be impatient (about the result)?"

The Messenger of Allah ﷺ said:

"The slave says: "I keep praying but my Lord does not answer my prayer". He gives up when his prayer is not answered immediately and he stops praying. (This is how he becomes impatient). (Muslim, Zikir, 92).

Likewise the prophet Zaccharia عليه السلام prayed ""**My Lord, do not leave me on my own....** (Anbiya, 21:89)

In saying so he asked for a son with the purpose of strengthening the religion, yet his prayer was only answered 40 years later in the form of the prophet Yahya عليه السلام.

❁

One time the Messenger of Allah saw a man in ritual prayer, who did not send blessings on the Prophet before he started supplicating. Upon this he said:

"This man was impatient (in a hurry)". Then he called that man to him and said as a caution to his entire community:

"Whenever one of you prays, let him first praise Allah Most High and then send blessings upon me. Then let him ask for whatever he so wishes" (Tirmidhi, Deavat, 64/3477).

❁

The Prophet Muhammad advised that a believer pray for his brother in religion either in his presence or in his absence. To Omar, who asked him for permission to perform the Lesser Pilgrimage he said:

"My brother, include us in your prayers, do not forget about us" (Tirmidhi, Deavat, 109/3562).

Omar explains how he felt when he heard these words:

"If they gave me the whole world I would not have been as happy as I was when I heard these words" (Abu Dawud, Vitir, 23/1498).

The Messenger of Allah has stated:

"The prayer of the Muslim that he makes for his brother in religion in his absence will be accepted. Whenever somebody prays for good for their brother, the angel that is on duty beside him prays for him: "May Allah accept your prayer and give you the same" (Muslim, Zikr 87, 88; Ibn-i Majah, Manasik, 5).

In that case we should pray for our Muslim brothers and sisters and ask them to pray for us.

What we need most in this fleeting world more than anything else is the state of *taqwa* (piety), and thus this is what we should ask for in our prayers. A man once came to the Messenger of Allah and said:

"O Messenger of Allah! I am about to take a journey, please pray for me".

The Prophet replied:

"May Allah bestow piety upon you" . The man said:

"A little more, o Messenger of Allah".

Allah's Messenger said:

"May Allah forgive your sins". The Companion said:

"A little more, may my father and mother be sacrificed for you o Messenger of Allah"

The Prophet ﷺ said:

"May Allah Most High make it easy for you to do good wherever you so happen to be" (Tirmidhi, Deavat, 44/3444).

❀

One day the Messenger of Allah read the following words of Abraham عليه السلام and the prayer of Jesus عليه السلام:

"My Lord! They have misguided many of mankind. If anyone follows me, he is with me..." (Ibrahim, 14:36).

"If You punish them, they are Your slaves. If you forgive them, You are the Almighty, the All-Wise". (Maide, 5:118).

After that he raised his hands and wept, pleadingly:

"O Allah! Protect my community, have mercy on my community". Upon this Almighty Allah said:

"O Gabriel! Though your Lord knows best (but in order for people to know), go to Muhammad and ask him why he is crying"

Gabriel went to him and the Messenger of Allah ﷺ told him that he was crying because he was worried about his community. When Gabriel returned to give this news Allah Most High said:

"O Gabriel! Go to Muhammad and tell him the good news that: "We will please you in regard to your community and We will never make you sad" (Muslim, Iman, 346).

So was our Prophet ever concerned with and merciful towards his community. As a response we need to deeply reflect on this *hadith* and ask ourselves how much we love him in return and if we do love him then we must ask ourselves how much of his *sun-*

159

nah have we applied to our lives and how much of his character have we adopted.

✸

Ibn-i Abbas 🙵 narrates:

"I once heard the Messenger of Allah 🙵 say the following supplication after the night time prayer:

"O Allah! I ask that You give me from Your Presence such mercy that with it You will guide my heart, regulate my affairs, and put order into my disorder. And that you will fill me with perfect faith, and bestow on my outer, good deeds and You will render my deeds pure and sincere, and inspire me with a suitable way to gain Your pleasure, and give us friends that will be familiar to me and protect me from all manner of evil.

O Allah! Give me such faith, such conviction that leaves no prospect for unbelief. Give me such mercy that with it I can reach a station in this world and the next, which is worthwhile in Your eyes.

O Allah! I ask you for salvation by Your grace in Your judgement of us. I implore of You a special rank worthy of the martyrs (who are close to You), I wish for the life of Your happy slaves, and I ask you for help against our enemies.

O Allah! Even though my understanding is limited and my deeds are few, I bring to your door my (worldly and otherworldly needs) and ask that You meet them. I am in need of Your Mercy, and I present my state to you.

O my Sustainer who judges all affairs and brings them about and who sees the needs of the hearts and offers the cure. As you have separated the seas, I ask that you separate me from the fire of Hell. I ask to be protected from destruction and from the torture of the grave.

O Allah! If there is any goodness in any of your slaves or any bounty that You have promised Your creatures that I have not been able to perceive or that has not been included in my intention and has thus remained outside of my petition, then O Lord of the Worlds, I ask You to bring it about and bestow it upon me out of Your mercy.

O Allah! O Possessor of the strong rope and correct path (such as the Qur'an and the religion). On the Day of Judgement on which you have promised the unbelievers hellfire , I ask you for safety against the hellfire, and on the day after which eternity begins I ask you for Paradise along with those angels that have attained to your Great Presence, together with those who made much bowing and prostration in this world, and who kept their promise. You are the Possessor of endless mercy, You are the Possessor of endless love, You do whatever You wish (however much the petitioners ask for and no matter how big You are capable of granting them all.) O Allah! Make us of those who have not strayed nor caused others to stray and make us guides of guidance who have attained to guidance. Make us vehicles for peace amongst our friends and enemies to our enemies. We love those who love you because of their love for You. We are enemies of those who go against You because of their animosity to You.

O Allah! This is our prayer. It is up to you whether You accept it with your gracious beneficence. This is our struggle and You are our support.

O Allah! Fill my heart with light, and my grave with light; place light in front of me, and light behind me; place light on my right and light on my left; place light above me and light below me; place light in my ears and light in my eyes, and light in my hair and my skin and my flesh and my blood and my bones.

O Allah increase my light, give me such light that it is worth all of what I have said and a light that will encompass everything that I could not say.

Glory be to the One Who is enveloped in dignity and Who has made Himself known by His dignity. I glorify the One who has enveloped Himself in greatness and who, for this reason, continually offers extensive bounty to His slaves. I glorify the One who is the only One worthy of glorification and holiness. I glorify the One who possesses majesty and beneficence. I glorify the One who possesses majesty and kindness. He is above all faults". (Tirmidhi, Deavat, 30/3419)

❀

One time people complained of the lack of rain to the Beloved Messenger of Allah ﷺ. Upon this, the Messenger of Allah asked that a pulpit be brought. The pulpit was assembled where the congregational, *eid* and funeral prayers were held (the *musalla*). A day was determined for when the people should gather there. The Prophet ﷺ set off when the redness of the sun had just appeared on the horizon. He arrived at the (*musalla*) and ascended the pulpit. He pronounced the *takbir* by saying "*Allahu Akbar*", praised Allah and then said:

"You have complained that your country is in drought and that rain has not fallen at its usual time and is late. Allah (glorified and majestic is he) has ordered you to supplicate to Him. He has promised that he will answer your prayer" and then the Prophet proceeded to make the following prayer:

"Praise belongs to the Lord of all the worlds. He is the Most Merciful, the Most Compassionate. He is the Master of the Day of Judgement. There is no god but Allah. He does as He pleases. O our Sustainer! You are Allah, and there is no other god but You. You are

rich. We are poor. Let the rains fall upon us. Make what you allow to fall be strength and power for us. Let it last us for a period".

After saying this he held up his hands. He lifted them up so high that the whites of his underarms could be seen. Then he turned his back on the people. His hands were still up in the air as he was doing this. Then he turned back to the people. He left the pulpit and prayed two cycles of prayer. Allah Most High immediately sent the clouds. It thundered and lightning struck. By the permission of Allah it began to rain. Before the Prophet had a chance to return to the Mosque it started to pour down rain. When the Messenger of Allah saw the congregation hurrying to take shelter he smiled and said:

"I bear witness that Allah is capable of everything and that I am the slave and Messenger of Allah" (Abu Dawud, Istiska, 2/1173).

After asking for rain from Allah Most High, our Prophet performed the special 'Prayer for Rain' and in this way turned to supererogatory prayer for the acceptance of his supplication.

❈

The Prophet's wife, Aisha has said:

"One night I awoke to find that Allah's Messenger was not beside me (in bed). I thought that he might have gone to another of his wives. I fumbled around looking for him when my hands touched his feet. Then I realised that Allah's Messenger was in prostration. I listened and heard him weeping and pleading as follows:

اَللّٰهُمَّ أَعُوذُ بِرِضَاكَ مِنْ سَخَطِكَ وَبِمُعَافَاتِكَ مِنْ عُقُوبَتِكَ وَأَعُوذُ بِكَ مِنْكَ
لَا أُحْصِى ثَنَاءً عَلَيْكَ أَنْتَ كَمَا اَثْنَيْتَ عَلَى نَفْسِكَ

"O Allah! I seek refuge in You from Your wrath. I seek refuge in Your forgiveness from your punishment. O Allah I seek refuge in You from You and from no other. I am incapable of truly praising You . You are as You have praised Yourself" (Muslim, Salat, 222; Tirmidhi, Deavat, 75/3493)

❋

Omar narrates:

"On the day of Badr, the Messenger of Allah looked at the polytheists and saw that they numbered a thousand men. His companions however numbered only 313[56]. He immediately turned towards the direction of the Ka'bah and raised his hands in prayer. He began to implore loudly to his Lord as follows:

"O Allah! Grant me what You have promised. O Allah. Grant me victory. O Allah. If you destroy this community of Islam then there will be nobody left on the face of the earth to worship you"

He continued supplicating with his hands raised until his cloak fell from his shoulders. Seeing this, Abu Bakr went to him and lifted it up over his shoulder and then said to him:

"O Messenger of Allah! Your prayer to Allah is sufficient. Allah Most High will definitely bring about His promise to you"

At that point Allah Most High, full of Honour and Majesty revealed the following verse:

"Remember when you called on your Lord for help and He responded to you: "I will reinforce you with a thousand angels riding rank after rank". (Anfal, 8:9)

And on that day too Allah Most High sent angels to help the believers. (Muslim, 58; Bukhari, Megazi, 4).

❋

---

56. See Bukhari, Megazi, 6; Tirmidhi, Siyer, 38/1598

There was a companion called Abu Mi'lak who was involved in trade in partnership with others. He was an honest and pious person. One time he had set off (on a journey) when his path was cut by an armed robber who said:

"Take out whatever you have. I am going to kill you"

"If your aim is to take my wealth then take it" said Abu Mi'lak

"I only want your life" said the robber. Abu Mi'lak said:

"In that case, allow me to perform the prayer. The robber said to him:

"Pray as much as you like". After he performed the prayer, Abu Mi'lak made the following supplication:

يَا وَدُودُ يَا ذَاالْعَرْشِ الْمَجِيدِ يَافَعَّالاً لِمَا يُرِيدُ أَسْأَلُكَ بِعِزَّتِكَ الَّتِى

لاَ تُرَامُ وَمُلْكِكَ الَّذِى لاَ يُضَامُ وَبِنُورِكَ الَّذِى مَلأَ اَرْكَانَ عَرْشِكَ

اَنْ تَكْفِيَنِى شَرَّ هَذَا (اللِّصِّ) يَا مُغِيثُ اَغِثْنِى

"O Beloved of hearts! O Possessor of the Mighty throne. O Allah, who does whatever He wills. In reverence for your unattainable dignity and your unobtainable kingdom and the light that envelops your throne, I ask that you protect me from the evil of this robber. O Allah who runs to everyone's aid, please come to my aid"

Abu Mi'lak repeated this prayer three times. As soon as he finished his prayer a cavalryman appeared with lance in hand at ear-level and killed the robber. The companion, who was saved by the grace of Allah, said to that cavalryman:

"Who are you? Allah used you as a means to help me"

165

The cavalrymen replied:

"I am a heavenly resident from the fourth heaven. When you made your first prayer I heard the doors of the heavens crack. At your second prayer I heard the clamour of the residents of the skies. When you prayed for the third time it was said: "Someone in trouble is asking for help. When I heard this I asked Allah to appoint me to kill the robber. Allah Most High accepted my plea and I came. Know this, that whoever does the ablution and prays four cycles of prayer and says this supplication will have their prayer accepted whether they are in trouble or not". (Ibn-i Hajar, al isaba, IV, 182)

The Prophet's wife, Ummu Salamah 🌸 was once asked:

"O mother of the believers! Which prayer did the Messenger of Allah 🌸 read most when he was with you?" She answered:

"Most of the time he would pray:

يَا مُقَلِّبَ الْقُلُوبِ ثَبِّتْ قَلْبِى عَلَى دِينِكَ

"O Allah who is the turner over of hearts! Make my heart firm upon your religion" (Tirmidhi, Deavat, 89/3522; Ahmad, IV, 182, VI, 91)

The Messenger of Allah made many prayers for the guidance of his community. For the guidance of the people of Yemen he prayed *"O Allah! Turn their hearts toward us"* (Tirmidhi, Menakib, 71/3934). The people of Taif turned him out of their town by stoning and insulting him in all manner of insults and continued to bring harm to the Muslims with their intense resistance until the 9th year of the *hijrah*. Yet for these people he prayed to Allah and sought refuge in Him: *"O my Sustainer! Grant guidance to the Thaqif. Send them to us".*

When the Prophet ﷺ sent Ali to Yemen to act as a judge he placed his hand upon the chest of his nephew, anxious at the responsibility of the burden placed upon him, and prayed as follows:

"O Allah! Guide his heart toward the truth, and make his tongue steady on the path of truth"

Ali ﷺ later said:

"After this prayer I never again hesitated when I had to judge between two people" (Ibn-i Maja, Ahkam, I).

During the halt of the Greater Pilgrimage, the Messenger of Allah ﷺ placed one of his hands on the halter of his camel and the other he raised and made a long supplication which expressed his servant hood and the sensitivity of his heart. A part of this beautiful supplication is as follows:

"O Allah! Praise be to you as You have praised Yourself and in a much better way than we could ever praise You. O Allah! My prayer, my worship, my life and my death are all for You. My return is to You alone.

O Allah! I seek refuge in You from the torture of the grave, from whisperings that swarm the heart, and from disorder in my affairs. O Allah! I seek refuge in You from the evil of disasters brought by strong winds.

O Allah! Bring light to my eyes, my ears and my heart. O Allah. Expand for me my breast. Make easy my task. O Allah. I seek refuge in You from health that turns into sickness, from your punishment

*that may strike suddenly and from your entire wrath. O Allah.
Guide me to the straight path. Forgive my past and my future (sins).*

*O Allah, the Creator of the heavens and the earth, who raises
the degrees and who bestows bounty. Different tongues overflowing
and resonating are all being raised to You and asking from You. My
wish from You is this: in this arena of examination, when the people
of the world have forgotten me I ask that You remember me.*

*O Allah! You hear my words. You see where I am. You know
everything about me, both open and secret. None of my affairs are
hidden from You. I am helpless and poor. I ask you for help and
mercy. I am afraid. I admit my faults. Just as the helpless asks from
You, so too do I ask. Just as a lowly sinner begs from You, so too do
I beg. However it is that a slave of Yours hangs his head low in Your
Presence, tears falling from his eyes, sacrificing his all for Your sake,
placing his face on the ground and prays to You, so too do I pray to
You. O my Sustainer! Do not deprive me of having my prayers
answered. Be Kind and Merciful to me, o the Best of those who are
asked and the most generous of givers"* [57]

What a sincere and concise prayer from the Messenger of
Allah, who was free of sin. This prayer demonstrates the state that
the heart should be in, in the presence of Allah Almighty...

❋

A part of the supplication made at Arafat by our righteous
predecessors (*salaf-i salihin*) is as follows:

"O Allah! Who can praise himself in front of You? O Allah!
My tongue is tied up in sin and I have no useful deed nor any
other intercessor, other than my hope in Your mercy, that will
bring me to You. O Allah. I know because of my faults that I have

---

57. See Ibn-i kathir, al Bidaya, V, 166-8; Haysami, III, 252; Ibn-i Kayyum, Zadu"l
Mead, Beirut 1995, II, 237

no place in Your presence and I am ashamed to apologise to You. However You are the most generous of the generous. O Allah. Even though I am not worthy of attaining to your mercy, please let your mercy reach me nonetheless. Because your mercy is broad enough to encompass all. O Allah. However big my faults are, they are small compared to your forgiveness. Please forgive them O Possessor of Generosity.

My Lord. If you only forgive your obedient slaves, then who can the sinners turn to?

My Lord. If you only show mercy and compassion to your pious slaves then who will the reprobates turn to for help?

I am in need of you at every instant. You, on the other hand, have no need of me. Only You, as my creator can forgive me. Allow me to return from where I am with all of my needs having been met, with my desires and my wishes come true.

O Allah, o possessor and ruler of the needs of those who ask. O Allah, who knows what is within those who are silent. O Allah, besides whom there is no other Sustainer to turn to for help. O Allah, besides whom there is no other creator who is to be feared. O Allah for whom there is no intercessor to apply to and no door-keeper whom one can bribe. O Allah, whose generosity and kindness increase as wants increase; and whose superior benevolence increases as needs multiply. O Allah! You are hospitable to each of your visitors. We too are Your visitors. Host us in Your Paradise.

O Allah! To each group is given a gift and to all askers is given what they ask for; offerings are made for all visitors. And to each person who hopes for it, reward is given to them. We have come, as a group, to Your Sacred House. We have halted at this great shrine[58] of Yours. We are present here in these holy places. Our

---

58. In Arabic *masha'ir*, which is a shrine for the ceremonies of the pilgrimage.

hope is to attain to the great reward and recompense that is with You. Do not let our hopes be in vain o Allah! [59]

Abu Umama narrates:

"The Messenger of Allah read many prayers but we were not able to memorise any of them. One day we said to him:

"O Messenger of Allah! You have read many prayers but we have been unable to learn all of them". The Prophet then said:

"Shall I teach you a prayer that encompasses all of those prayers? Say as follows:

اَللّٰهُمَّ إِنَّا نَسْأَلُكَ مِنْ خَيْرِ مَاسَأَلَكَ مِنْهُ نَبِيُّكَ مُحَمَّدٌ صَلَّى اللهُ عَلَيْهِ وَسَلَّمَ

وَنَعُوذُ بِكَ مِنْ شَرِّ مَااسْتَعَاذَكَ مِنْهُ نَبِيُّكَ مُحَمَّدٌ صَلَّى اللهُ عَلَيْهِ وَسَلَّمَ

وَأَنْتَ الْمُسْتَعَانُ وَعَلَيْكَ الْبَلَاغُ وَلَا حَوْلَ وَلَا قُوَّةَ إِلَّا بِاللهِ

"O Allah. We beg of You all the good things that Your Prophet Muhammad sought from You and we seek Your protection against all the evils that Your Prophet Muhammad sought Your protection. You are the only Helper who is asked for help. You are the One who will allow man to reach his aim in both this world and the next. There is no strength to avoid sin, nor no power to perform worship other than from Allah!"

Anas narrates:

"The Messenger of Allah once visited a sick person who had lost much weight and asked:

59. See Ghazalli, Ihya Ulumi"d- Din, Beirut, 1990, I, 337-8; Beyhaki, ShuAbu'l Iman, II, 25-6

"Were you praying for anything from Allah or did you ask for anything from Him?" The sick person replied:

"Yes. I used to pray "O Allah! Give me the punishment now that you would have given me in the afterlife!"

The Messenger of Allah 🕋 said:

"Glory be to Allah! You do not have the power to withstand this. Couldn't you have prayed as follows:

رَبَّنَا آتِنَا فِي الدُّنْيَا حَسَنَةً وَفِي الْآخِرَةِ حَسَنَةً وَقِنَا عَذَابَ النَّارِ

"... O our Sustainer! Give us good in this world and give us good in the hereafter and protect us from the punishment of the fire" (Baqara, 2:201).

The man then said this prayer and was cured. (Muslim, Zikr, 23; Tirmidhi, Deavat, 71/3487)

Thus we must be very careful about what we ask for from Allah and we must comply with the etiquette of supplication. We should always ask for goodness and well being from Allah.

❁

According to a narration by Ali 🕋 a contracted slave once came to him and said:

"I am not able to repay my debt, help me". He said to him:

"Shall I teach you a prayer that the Messenger of Allah 🕋 taught me? As long as you continue saying it, Allah Most High will help you pay back your debt even if it as great as the Mountain of Thabir" and he read the following prayer:

اَللّٰهُمَّ اكْفِنِي بِحَلَالِكَ عَنْ حَرَامِكَ وَاغْنِنِي بِفَضْلِكَ عَمَّنْ سِوَاكَ

"O Allah! Bestow on me lawful provision and protect me from the unlawful! By Your grace do not make me dependent on any other than You" (Tirmidhi, Deavat, 110/3563).

❋

When Sultan Murad I entered the plains of Kosovo he was met with a fierce storm which left dust in its wake. Not a thing could be seen. That night was the Night of Beraat (Forgiveness). After praying two cycles of prayer, Murad Han made the following prayer, tears flowing down his cheeks:

"O my Sustainer! If this storm has appeared due to the sins of this helpless slave of yours then please do not punish my innocent soldiers with it. O Allah! They came here for the sole purpose of exalting Your Name and propagating Islam.

O my Sustainer! You have not deprived me of victory all of these years. You have always accepted my prayers. Again I turn to You, so accept my prayer. Give us some rain. Let it lift this dust storm. Let us see clearly the faces of the unbelievers and let us do combat face to face"

O my Sustainer! Wealth and this slave too are both Yours. I am a helpless slave. You know best my intention and my secrets. My aim is not wealth nor property. I wish only to gain Your pleasure.

O my Sustainer! Do not destroy these believing soldiers and defeat them at the hands of the unbelievers. Give them such victory that all of the Muslims can celebrate. And if You so wish let this slave of Yours be the sacrifice for that feast.

O my Sustainer! Do not make me the cause of the destruction of so many Muslim soldiers. Help them and grant them victory. I would sacrifice my life for them if only to be accepted by You into the community of martyrs. I am willing to surrender my spirit for these soldiers of Islam...You have made me a soldier. Bestow martyrdom on me now through your Grace and beneficence... Amen!"

After this sincere, heartfelt entreaty the Sultan began to recite from the Qur'an with extraordinary calm. It wasn't long before the clouds of mercy appeared. A heavy rain poured over the plains of Kosovo. The winds stopped blowing. The dust disappeared...

The enemy was then attacked. The battle that lasted for eight hours ended in victory.

As Murad Han was walking amongst the wounded and martyrs of the battle field, a wounded Serbian shoulder stood up and said:

"Let me go. I'm going to the Sultan to kiss his hand and become Muslim". The Serbian soldier who was pretending to be wounded made as if to kiss the hand of Sultan Murad. He then quickly plunged a sword he had hidden under his arm into the chest of the Sultan. And there the prayer of Sultan Murad was answered in the most perfect way and he was blessed with martyrdom...

❋

In conclusion, supplication has a central position in the life of worship and servant hood. This is because one of the things Allah is most pleased with is that the slave perceives his helplessness and raises his hands to present his case to his Lord and to pray and seek refuge in Him. This is why Allah Most High punishes the one who refuses to lower himself and disdains from praying and does not humble himself in asking for anything.

The Holy Qur'an says:

"Say: "What has My Lord to do with you if you do not call on Him?" (Furqan, 25:77)

Supplication is thus the key to the gates of mercy, the weapon of the believer, the pillar of religion and the light of the heavens and the earth. Whoever has had the gates of prayer opened for them has also had opened for them the gates of goodness, wisdom and mercy. The one who wishes to have their prayer accepted in times of distress and difficulty must make sure to pray much during times of plenty and comfort. Great souls are those who live their lives in a constant state of prayer.

e. Humility and deep reverence (khushu)

Khushu indicates the state of the heart being filled with the love and fear of Allah and the limbs finding peace and tranquillity as a result of these feelings.

Khushu, whose essence is in the heart but whose manifestations appear in the body, has two aspects:

The aspect that is of the heart is when it perceives its nothingness in the face of its Sustainer's magnificence and majesty. The *nafs* too then submits to the command of Allah, and attains to superior manners and feelings of reverence and respect. The outer aspect is when the effect of these feelings brings about dignity and tranquillity in the limbs of the body. For instance to stop the eyes from wandering when one is performing the prayer and to look at the place of prostration...

The best example of how to apply *khushu* to one's life and one's worship can be seen in the life of the Prophet ﷺ and his Blessed Companions. Allah's Messenger ﷺ did not evaluate any stage of his life without relating it the hereafter. He drew attention to the importance of embodying oneself in a spiritual state during worship as one would at the last breath.

A Companion once approached the Messenger of Allah ﷺ and said:

"O Messenger of Allah! Give me some advice, only let it be short and concise". Upon this the Prophet ﷺ said:

"Perform your salat (prayer) as one who is saying farewell to his life. Do not utter any word that you will have to apologise for. Do not envy what others have" (Ibn-i Majah, Zuhd, 15; Ahmad, V, 412).

Worship is only of any worth when it is performed in a state of vigilance, deep reverence (*khushu*) and reflection. The most important virtue of the Blessed Companions and those righteous believers who followed them was this consistent character in their heart.

Abdullah bin Mas'ud ﷺ would tell his friends:

"You pray more and struggle more than the companions. But they are yet more virtuous than you"

When it was asked of him:

"What makes them more virtuous than us?" he answered:

"They were more abstaining from the world and more deter-mined for the hereafter than you". (Ibnu'l Jawzi, Sifatu's Safwe, Beirut 1979, I, 420).

The state of deep reverence during prayer is so important that the salvation of the slave occurs through this door. The Holy Qur'an says in Chapter *Mu'minun*:

"It is the believers who are successful: those who are humble in their *salat*" (Mu'minun, 23:1-2).

Our Prophet also informs us of how the slave will be treated according to how well he observed the prayer:

"A slave performs the prayer, however, only one-tenth or one-ninth, or one-eighth, or one-seventh, or one-sixth, or one-fifth, or one-fourth, or one third or half of it is recorded for him". (Abu Dawud, Salat, 123-4/796).

That is, there is reward for the prayer of the slave only if it is performed with reverence and attentiveness.

Yet again our Sustainer explains how the believer can perform the prayer with reverence as follows:

"Seek help in steadfastness and *salat*. But that is a very hard thing, except for the humble: those who are aware that they will meet their Lord and that they will return to Him" (Baqara, 2:45-6)

That is, one will have reached a state of true *khushu* or deep reverence if one performs the prayer with the certainty that one day they will eventually appear in the presence of their Lord and have to account for everything that they did.

As this state of awe during the prayer continues it will in time extend to the whole of the believers life. This is why Jaluluddin Al Rumi explains the verse **"those who do salat and are constant in it"** (Ma'arij, 70:22-3) as follows:

"Your state after prayer should be the same as your state during the prayer".

In order to be able to attain to this state it is necessary to become like the Messenger of Allah 🕮 by benefiting from his exalted character and by forming in the heart a sincere and deep bond with him. As he said:

"...Allah loves the heart that is full of awe, sorrow, and compassion and which teaches goodness to the people and calls to the obedience of Allah. And He abhors the heart that occupies itself with vain things, which spends its entire night in sleep even though it does not

know whether or not its soul will be returned to it, and remembers Allah very little" (Deylemi, I, 158)

Scenes of Virtue

Abdullah bin Shihhir ﷺ informs us of the deep reverence of the Prophet as follows:

"One time I had gone to the Messenger of Allah ﷺ. He was praying and crying and it sounded like his chest was boiling". (Abu Dawud, Salat, 156-7, 904; Ahmad, IV, 25,26).

It is vital that one pays attention to the formal rules (*fiqh*) of the prayer. However, as the *hadiths* state we must also take particular care to be scrupulous about our spiritual state. *Fiqh* prepares the slave in terms of purity, ablution and cleanliness, whereas purity of the heart, or *khushu* (deep reverence) allows the believer to attain to peaceful presence and perceptiveness of the heart and "divine meeting".

❀

The Prophet ﷺ expressed the necessity of performing the prayer in a state of great awe and entreaty to Almighty Allah:

"The prayer (salat) is performed in cycles (rakats) of two. At the end of each rakat the believer sits for the tashahhud[60]. Salat is deep reverence, and an expression of one's humility and lowliness before Allah. (At the end) you raise your hands to your Sublime Sustainer with the palms turned towards your face and you plead: "O my Sustainer! O my Sustainer!". The prayer of the one who does not do this is deficient. (Tirmidhi, Salat, 166/385).

❀

---

60. Tashahhud is the part of the ritual prayer when the believer sits and recites the tashahhud prayer (translator's note).

Aisha 🌸 narrates:

"Abu Jahm 🌸 once presented a gift of an embroidered, elegant dress to the Messenger of Allah 🌸 who performed the prayer with it. When he finished he said:

"Give this dress back to Abu Jahm. My eyes were distracted by the embroidery on it. It almost made me lose my presence in the prayer". (Muwatta, Salat, 67; Bukhari, Salat, 14).

❀

The Messenger of Allah 🌸 taught his community the rules of Hajj by personally applying them during the Farewell Hajj. He explained that it was necessary in particular to have deep reverence during Hajj just as with other forms of worship.

And so it was that the Prophet was once returning to Muzdalifa from Arafat on the Day of Arafat. He heard some people behind him screaming and shouting and hitting their camels and the camels were bellowing. He pointed his staff at them and said:

"O people! (Slow down) Be steady. You cannot gain reward by rushing" (Bukhari, Hajj, 94; Muslim, Hajj, 268).

❀

Ali 🌸 narrates:

"The Prophet once saw a man playing with his beard during the prayer. Seeing this he said:

"If his heart had felt any khushu (pious reverence) so too would all of his limbs" (Ali al-Muttaki, VIII, 197/22530).

❀

Aisha 🌸 narrates that her mother Ummu Ruman 🌸, once said to her:

"Once when I was praying I kept swaying to and fro. When Abu Bakr saw this state of mine he chided me so much that I almost interrupted my prayer. After he said:

"The Messenger of Allah has said:

"*Whenever one of you stands to pray let every part of him remain still and in deep reverence. Let him not sway back and forth like the Jews. For the stillness of the limbs in prayer is one of the aspects that completes the prayer*" (Alusi, Ruhu'l Ma'ani, Beirut ts., XVIII, 3).

❁

Despite being given great wealth and kingdom, the prophet Solomon 🕮 was able to free his heart from attachment to the world and live a life of servant hood, being in a continual state of pious reverence, humility and fervour. This virtue of his has been explained as follows:

"*Despite having been given wealth, Solomon never once in his life lifted his head up towards the heavens out of the deep reverence he felt for Allah*" (Ibn-i Abi Shayba, al Musannaf, Beirut, Daru'l-Fikr 1989, VIII, 118).

❁

Abdullah bin Abu Bakr 🕮 narrates:

"Abu Talha was once praying in his garden. A bird called 'Dubsi' tried to fly out of the garden and searched for a place to get out. This amused Abu Talha and his eyes followed the bird for a second. Then he turned back to his prayer but he forgot how many cycles he had prayed. Thinking that this bird became a cause of distraction and ruined his state of reverence he then went to the Prophet and told him what happened:

"O Messenger of Allah! I give this bird of mine in charity. You may use it as you wish and give it to whomever you wish" (Muwatta, Salat, 69)

How exquisite is the following event which shows the deep reverence of the Companions during prayer.

"One time when the Prophet was returning to Madina after an expedition he stopped along the way. He turned to his Companions and asked:

"Who will keep watch tonight?"

Ammar bin Yasir 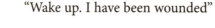 from the Emmigrants and Abbad bin Bishr from the Helpers immediately responded:

"We will o Messenger of Allah"

Abbad then asked Ammar:

"Which part of the night would you like to keep watch over; the beginning or the end?" Ammar replied:

"I would like to keep watch at the end" and then went to sleep on his side. Abbad then began to perform the prayer. At that point a polytheist appeared. When he saw a dark figure standing he realised it must be a guard and he aimed an arrow at him. The arrow hit Abbad. Abbad removed the arrow and continued to pray. The man aimed again a second and third time and hit him each time. Each time Abbad would stand upright, take out the arrow and continue to pray. Then he bowed down and went into prostration. After he ended his prayer he woke up his friends and said:

"Wake up. I have been wounded"

Ammar immediately sprung up. When the polytheist saw them he realised that he had been seen and escaped. When Ammar saw Abbad bleeding profusely he said:

"Glory be to Allah! Why did not you wake me up when the first arrow was thrown?"

Abbad gave the following awesome reply which showed his passion and enthusiasm for the prayer and the deep reverence of his worship:

"I was reading a chapter from the Qur'an. I did not want to end my prayer without finishing it. But when the arrows kept coming without a break I stopped reading and bowed down. I swear to Allah if I hadn't been afraid of losing my position of commander appointed to me by the Messenger of Allah I would have rather died then have that chapter interrupted"

❁

Asma ⬡, the daughter of Abu Bakr ⬡, was once asked by her grandson Abdullah:

"Grandma! What did the Companions of the Prophet used to do when they listened to the Qur'an?"

Asma ⬡ replied:

"Tears would flow from their eyes and their bodies would shudder just as mentioned in the Qur'an. (Bayhaki, ShuAbu'l Iman, II, 365).

Almighty Allah describes his servants who read the Qur'an with deep reverence as follows:

"When it (the Qur'an) is recited to them, ... weeping, they fall to the ground in prostration, and it increases them in humility". (Isra, 17:109)

"The skins of those who fear their Lord tremble at it (the Qur'an) and then their skins and hearts yield softly to the remembrance of Allah" (Az Zumar, 3:23)

❈

One time during a battle an arrow lodged itself into the foot of Ali ﷺ. They couldn't take it out due to the pain. Ali said to them:

"Let me perform the prayer, then you can take it out"

They did as he said. They were then able to remove it easily without any difficulty. When Ali, who felt no pain whatsoever, ended his prayer he asked them:

"What did you do?"

They replied:

"We took the arrow out"

❈

Veysel Karani was once asked by his mother:

"My son. How are you able to worship for an entire night until morning? How do you bear it?"

That great friend of Allah responded:

"O my beautiful mother! I perform my worship with great care and precision. With deep reverence my heart expands to such a degree that just as I do not realise what it is to feel fatigue, I feel cut off from the world and all manner of feelings related to my body. And then before I know it, it is morning..."

"What is this state of *khushu* Uways?"

"*Khushu* is when your body is unaware of even a spear piercing it".

❈

According to a narration whenever Zayn al Abideen rose to take his ablution his face would turn pale and whenever he began to pray his legs would shake. When he was asked the reason he said:

"Are you not aware of Whose presence I am entering? (Abu Nuaym, Hilya, III, 133).

One time when he was praying his house caught fire. However he remained unaware of this. When he finished his prayer and was told of the situation they asked him:

"What was it that made you fail to notice that your house was on fire?".

Zayn al Abideen replied:

"The fire that awaits mankind in the hereafter made me forget the fire of this world".

❁

The prayer of Muslim bin Yesar was of a similar nature. One time he was praying in a mosque in Basra. Suddenly the mosque came falling down. However Muslim bin Yesar remained unaware of this event and continued his prayer. When he finished they asked him:

"The mosque came crashing down yet you did not move an inch. What is this state?"

Muslim bin Yesar asked in surprise:

"Did the mosque really come tumbling down?" as further proof that he truly did not feel any of it during his prayer.

❁

A friend of Allah narrates:

"I was once praying the afternoon prayer behind Zunnun-i Misri. When that blessed Saint said "*Allahu Akbar* (Allah is the

Greatest), the word "*Allah*" had such a great impact on him that it was as if there was no life left in his body. He froze and stood there just like that. When he said the word "*Akbar*" my heart crumbled to pieces from the majesty of the word.

❖

Whenever Amir bin Abdullah stood to pray he would disconnect from the (outside) world completely and nothing that was other than Allah could damage his state of pious reverence.

"I would prefer spears to pierce my body rather than be aware of other people's speech and actions during my prayer" he used to say.

❖

Bahauddin Nakshiband ﷺ was once asked:

"How can a slave gain pious reverence during the prayer?" He answered:

"There are four conditions:

1.   His provision must be lawful

2.   He must distance himself from heedlessness while performing the ablution

3.   He must realise his presence (before Allah) with the first *takbir*.

4.   He must never forget Allah outside of prayer. That is, his state of presence, tranquillity and abstaining from sin must continue after his prayer has ended"

❖

In short, *khushu* is to carry out Allah's commands with ardour and to meticulously refrain from what He has forbidden. *Khushu* (pious reverence), *taqwa* (God-consciousness), *ikhlas* (sincerity), and *ihsan* (beneficence) are similar in their states and meanings. The source of all of these is love for Allah. Love of Allah is an indicator of the state of the heart of the believer. This spiritual state manifests itself as worship that is carried out with pious reverence and perfection of one's actions.

Pious reverence must fill our hearts at every instant of our lives and while we are carrying out all forms of worship, in particular the prayer. And it should be reflected to those around us from our limbs as a state of peace and tranquillity.

7. To be familiar with the Holy Qur'an

The Holy Qur'an is a teacher of guidance that shows us the true path. It is mercy for the believers, and a cure for the maladies of the heart. At the same time it is a divine mentor that takes mankind out of the darkness and brings him into the light and closer to Allah with His permission.

The Holy Qur'an is a divine decree that informs man of the purpose of the creation of all things. It proclaims the wisdom in the creation of mankind and commands that life be lived in a manner suitable to the divine order present throughout the universe.

Almighty Allah states:

"Allah has sent down the Supreme Discourse, a Book consistent in its frequent repetitions. The skins of those who fear their Lord tremble at it   and then their skins and hearts yield softly to the remembrance of Allah. That is Allah's guidance by which He guides whoever He wills. And no one can guide those whom Allah misguides". (Az Zumar, 39:23)

This verse describes the kind of relationship our heart should have with the Qur'an.

The degree of our *taqwa* is related to our Quranic ethos which manifests itself in the form of a Quranic character consisting of sincerity in our worship, beauty in our behaviour, and depth of our hearts.

The Holy Qur'an is the most reliable handle one can hold onto. Allah Most High has extended it to those slaves of His who want to gain His good pleasure and who want to be saved from evil and from eternal punishment. Those who hold onto it are saved, and will be raised and dignified; those who reject it will be brought down low; they will be debased and they will stray far from the straight path.

The Holy Qur'an is a spiritual banquet that Allah Most High has prepared as an offering for His slaves. Those who accept this invitation from their Lord and partake of the feast will taste the pleasure of endless bounties which result in peace, happiness and joy.

The true dignity and honour of the human being depends on the degree to which they carry out its commands and perfect themselves with its character. That is, mankind can only attain to the dignity and honour that is in accordance with the purpose of his creation, to the degree that he envelops himself in the spirituality and prosperity of the Qur'an and obeys the divine commands. Almighty Allah commands us to reflect on life and events with the logic of the Qur'an by having properly comprehended it. Thus the mind, which can be a source of both happiness and dissipation, needs the direction offered through revelation.

If we did not have a door of reflection opened up for us by the Qur'an, we would be deprived of perceiving and expressing many truths. Accordingly thinking deeply about the contents of the Qur'an will ensure the discovery of many paths of goodness.

It is necessary to become familiar with the Qur'an and to occupy oneself with it much in order to properly learn the Islamic character.

It is stated in a hadith:

"If anyone of you loves to supplicate and converse (implore and speak with) your Lord, let him read the Qur'an with his heart fully attendant and attentive. (Suyuti, I, 13/360).

"Read the Qur'an! Because on the Day of Judgement, the Qur'an will appear as an intercessor for the one who read it" (Muslim, Musafirin, 252,253; Ahmad, V, 249, 251).

"On the Day of Judgement a crown will be placed on the heads of the parents of those who read the Qur'an and act according to it. The light from this crown is more beautiful than the light from the sun that would light up a house were it to be put into it. In that case, can you imagine the light of one who acts according to the Qur'an?" (Abu Dawud, Vitir, 14/1453).

To become very well-acquainted with the Qur'an is a righteous deed that Allah is pleased and content with. The Messenger of Allah ﷺ said:

"Allah Most High is pleased with nothing more than the recitation of the Qur'an by a prophet with a beautiful voice, loudly and with teganni[61]" (Bukhari, Fadailu'l Qur'an 19, Tawheed 32; Muslim, Musafirin 232-234).

---

61. Teganni has the following meanings of embellishing the Qur'an, the most beautiful of words, in a manner suitable to it and with a beautiful voice. It is to emphasise (make obvious) the joy and sorrow in one's voice when reading it and to read it clearly and with a loud voice.For a detailed explanation see M.Yasar Kandemir, Ismail Lutfi Cakan, Rasit Kucuk, Riyadhu-s Saliheen – Translation and Commentary, Istanbul 2001, V, 118).

"Allah listens to nothing as much as He listens to His slave who performs two rakats of prayer at night and who (reads the Qur'an). The mercy of Allah is spread over the head of the slave for the time that he spends in prayer. The slave can never approach Allah more than at the time they are one with the Qur'an" (Tirmidhi, Fadailu'l Qur'an, 17/2911).

It has been said that those people who forget the chapters of the Qur'an that they have memorised because they have not spent enough time with it, incur great sin (Abu Dawud, Salat, 16/461). Somebody who does not have even a small amount of the Qur'an in their heart is like a rundown house[62]

The Messenger of Allah ﷺ has said:

"The hearts rust just as iron rusts". His Companions asked:

"What is the polish for this Messeger of Allah?"

The Messenger of Allah ﷺ replied:

"Reading the Book of Allah much and remembering Allah much". (Ali al-Muttaki, II, 241).

On another day the Messenger of Allah advised his Companions:

"Give what is due to your eyes from worship"

"What is it that is due to our eyes o Messenger of Allah?" they asked him.

The Prophet replied:

"To look at the Mushaf (pages of the Qur'an), to reflect on what is in them and to take lesson from the subtleties within" (Suyuti, I, 39).

Another time the Prophet ﷺ said:

---

62. Tirmidhi, Fadai'ul Qur'an, 18/2913; Darimi, Fadail'ul Qur'an, 1

"For sure there are those amongst people who are close to Allah"

When he was asked:

"O Messenger of Allah! Who are they?" he replied:

"They are the people of the Qur'an, the people of Allah, and Allah's special slaves". (Ibn-i Majah, Mukaddima, 16).

The Prophet Muhammad ﷺ was especially pleased when people would get together in an effort to read and understand the Qur'an. He said about these people:

"...If a group of people gather together in one of the houses of Allah to read the book of Allah and discuss it and try to understand and comprehend it, there falls upon them a type of tranquillity and mercy envelops them. The angels surround them. Allah Most High mentions them in the company of those around him. For the one who has strayed behind (by neglecting his deeds), his lineage will not advance him..." (Muslim, Zikir, 38; Ibn-i Majah, Mukaddima, 17).

In that case we must increase the bonds of our hearts to the Holy Qur'an for the happiness of both of our worlds. We must read and understand it, feel it in our hearts, and struggle to apply its rulings in all sincerity.

Scenes of Virtue

The Prophet ﷺ used to read the Holy Qur'an in a manner befitting it and ponder deeply on its meaning and follow its commands without delay. He would read the Qur'an with wholeheartedly, truly feeling and living it. While reading, if he came to a verse which glorified Allah he would absolve Allah of all defects and faults) by saying 'SubhanAllah' (Glory be to Allah). When he came across verses about supplication he would pray to Allah.

When he came to verses which mentioned seeking refuge in Allah he would immediately seek refuge in Allah. (See Muslim, Musafirin, 203; Nasai, Kıyamu"l Layl, 25).

The Prophet would regularly read from the Qur'an every day.[63] Aws bin Huzayfa ؛ who was from the tribe of Thakif that came to Madina narrates:

"One night, the Messenger of Allah did not appear before us for a long time after the night time prayer.

"O Messenger of Allah! Why did you wait so long to come out?" we asked him. The Prophet replied:

"*I have made it a duty incumbent upon myself to read a* hizb *(1/60th) of the Qur'an every day. I did not want to come out until I had completed it*".

When it was morning we asked the Companions:

"How do you divide up the Qur'an to read it?" They answered:

"We call the first three chapters one *hizb*, then the next 5 chapters the second *hizb*, then the next 7, the next 9, the next 11, the next 13 are each a *hizb*. Lastly the chapter Kaf and the chapters that follow it are another *hizb*. Thus we read the Qur'an in 7 parts". (Ahmad, IV, 9; Ibn-i Majah, Salat, 178).

Abdullah ibn-i Mas'ud ؛ relates:

"One time the Prophet ؛ commanded me:

"*O Ibn-i Mas'ud! Recite the Qur'an to me*". I replied:

"O Messenger of Allah! How can I recite the Qur'an to you when it has been revealed to you?"

---

63. Muslim, Musafirin, 142; Ahmad, IV, 9İ Ibn-i Majah, Salat, 178)

Allah's Messenger said:

"*I like to hear the Qur'an being recited by others*".

I then began to read from the chapter *Nisa*. When I came to the verse:

"**How then, [will the sinners fare on Judgement Day] when We shall bring forward witnesses from within every community, and bring thee (O Prophet) as witness against them**" (An Nisa, 4:41) the Messenger of Allah said:

"*That will do*".

At that point I looked to see tears like pearls falling from his eyes" (Bukhari, Tafsir, 4/9; Muslim, Musafirin, 247).

What a beautiful scene that demonstrates the mercy the Prophet had for his community...

❀

One day when Aisha 🌸 was late in appearing before Allah's Messenger he asked her the reason. She replied that she wanted to listen to the Qur'an and that is why she was late:

"O Messenger of Allah! There was a man at the mosque. I have never heard someone reciting the Qur'an more beautifully than him". Upon this the Messenger of Allah went to the mosque and saw that that man was Salim 🌸. He said:

"*I praise Allah that there is someone like this amongst my community.* (Ibn-i Majah, Ikamah, 176; Ahmad, VI, 165; Hakim, III, 250/5001).

❀

A Companion once asked the Messenger of Allah 🌸:

"O Messenger of Allah! Which deed is the most pleasing to Allah?" The Beloved Prophet replied:

"The deeds of *hal* and *murtehil*".

"And what are *hal* and *murtehil*?". He answered:

"Reading the Qur'an from beginning to end and then once fin-ished, starting again from the beginning". (Tirmidhi, Kiraat, 11/2948).

It is now common practice that once an entire reading of the Qur'an has been completed, one then reads the last three chapters of the Qur'an and then begins again and recites the opening chap-ter, *al Fatiha*, and then the first five verses of the next chapter, *Baqara*. This is done in order to attain to the virtue that is men-tioned in this hadith.

Thus a new reading is commenced and a righteous deed acceptable by Allah is carried out.

❋

Allah's Messenger ﷺ would give the utmost importance to the Qur'an and he loved those of his Companions who did likewise.

One time the Prophet was going to send a detachment great in number. He had them read Qur'an. Each of them recited as much of the verses of Allah that they had memorised. The Prophet approached the youngest of the Companions and asked him:

"O such and such. What have you memorised?" He replied:

"I have memorised such and such chapters and chapter *Baqara*". The Prophet said:

"Have you memorised chapter Baqara?"

When the reply was "yes" he said:

"Off you go. You are their leader. This chapter comprises almost the whole of religion"

One of the leaders from the group said:

"O Messenger of Allah. My fear of not being able to apply what is in *Baqara* has prevented me from memorising it".

Upon this the Messenger of Allah 🌸 said:

"*Learn the Qur'an, read it, have others read it and act by it. Because the one who learns the Qur'an, and reads and acts upon it, is like a bottle of musk which spreads its scent everywhere. The one who learns the Qur'an, but who sleeps (that is, is behind in his service of the Qur'an) is like a bottle of musk with its lid tightly closed*". (Tirmidhi, Fadailu'l Qur'an, 2/2876).

This event describes the degree of physical and spiritual learning of the one who reads and lives by the chapter *Baqara*. Also with this *hadith* the Prophet 🌸 announces the responsibility of the believers in becoming familiar with and teaching the Qur'an.

❀

After the Companions had learnt 10 verses from the Messenger of Allah, they would not move onto memorising another ten before they had fully comprehended the commands and wisdom of the first ten and applied them to their lives. They applied the knowledge found in the Qur'an and they reached a state of perfection also with the wisdom contained within it. (Ahmad, V, 410).

Omar 🌸 said:

"I completed the chapter *Baqara* in twelve years and as gratitude for that I sacrificed a camel" (Kurtubi, al-Jami li- ahkami'l Qur'an, Beirut 1985, I, 40).

Abdullah bin Omar 🌸 completed *Baqara* in eight years. (Muwatta, Qur'an, 11).

Reading the Qur'an is of any value only if it is lived and taught to others.

❀

The representatives of the tribe of Thaqif, who had come to see the Prophet had left Othman bin Abi'l As to mind the animals as he was the youngest of them. When the representatives had returned and fell asleep under the heat of the midday sun Othman, went to the Prophet and asked him questions about religion, and listened to the Qur'an and learned it. In this way he had been able to read and memorise some chapters from the Prophet.

Whenever, Othman who had secretly made a pact with the Prophet and became Muslim before his representative friends, would come to learn the Qur'an, if the Messenger of Allah was not available, he would either go to Abu Bakr, or Ubayy bin Ka'b and ask them what he had to ask and learn what he wanted to learn.

This pleased the Messenger of Allah greatly who loved him very much. When the representatives of Thaqif wished to return to their country they said:

"O Messenger of Allah! Will you make one of us a leader?"

The Prophet made Othman bin Abi'l As their leader even though he was the youngest amongst them. (Ibn-I Sa'd, V, 508; Ibn-I Hisham, IV, 185; Ahmad, IV, 218).

The Quranic verses, which were revealed for various reasons and one after the other, were a source of indescribable happiness for the Messenger of Allah and his Companions, and would increase their determination and refresh their heart's bond with Allah. They had become so much at one with revelation that their sorrow was compounded when the revelation was interrupted with the death of the Prophet.

We can see this striking example of this love in the following event:

After the death of the Messenger of Allah ﷺ Abu Bakr said to Omar ﷺ:

"Stand up and let's go to Ummu Ayman, one who was very dear and near to Allah's Messenger. Let us visit her as the Prophet used to do"

When they arrived at Ummu Ayman's ﷺ she began to cry. They asked her:

"Why are you crying? Don't you know that the bounty with Allah is much better for the Prophet?"

Ummu Ayman replied:

"That is not why I am crying. Of course I know that the bounty with Allah is much better for the blessed Prophet. I am crying because the revelation has come to an end".

These words that expressed the longing for Divine revelation touched Abu Bakr ﷺ and Omar ﷺ and they also began to cry along with Ummu Ayman ﷺ. (Muslim, Fadailu's Sahabe, 103).

❈

The Companions of the Prophet would read the Qur'an often, and would not wish a day to pass in which they had not read it or looked at its pages. They would begin their day with the Qur'an and would advise those who had problems with their eyes to look at its pages. (Haysami, VII, 165).

Othman, who was honoured with the title of 'Jami'ul Qur'an', or the Compiler of the Qur'an due to his service to it, had outworn two scripts because he was so preoccupied with it" (Kettani, Nizamu'l Hukumeti'n Nabawwiyya (at- Teratibu'l Idariyye), Beirut 1996, II, 197).

❈

Usayd bin Hudayr ﷺ narrates:

"One night I was reading chapter *Baqara*. My horse was tied up near me. At one point, it rose up on its two back legs. I stopped reading; the horse calmed down. I began to read again, and the horse reared up again. In fact I was afraid that the horse was going to stomp on my son Yahya, so I went next to it. At that point when I looked up at the sky I saw something that looked like candles. Then they rose up towards the sky and disappeared.

When it was morning I told the Messenger of Allah ﷺ what had happened. He said:

"Read o Usayd, read"... Then he said:

"O Usayd, do you know what it was that you saw?"

"No" I replied. The Messenger of Allah said:

"They were angels which had come to listen to you recite the Qur'an. If you had continued to read they would have listened to you until the morning. They would not have remained invisible to the people who would have been able to see them" (Bukhari, Fadailu'l Qur'an, 15, Menakib 25; Muslim, Musafirin 241-242).

One day the Messenger of Allah ﷺ addressed a lover of the Qur'an, Ubayy bin Ka'b as follows:

"Allah Most High commanded me to tell you to read the chapter "Lam yakunillethine kafaru"

Ubayy bin Ka'b ﷺ asked:

"Did Allah Most High mention my name?"

The Messenger of Allah ﷺ replied:

"yes".

Ubayy bin Ka'b was so touched by this divine compliment that he began to weep profusely. (Bukhari, Menakibu'l Ansar 16, Tafsir 98/1, 3; Muslim, Misafirin, 246).

Ubayy bin Ka'b was at the head of the list of *hafiz* (those who have memorised the Qur'an completely). He was one of those four fortunate ones about whom the Prophet said *"Learn the Qur'an from one of these four people"*. He was the one who read the Qur'an in the most beautiful way and the most often. (Bukhari, Fedail'ul Qur'an, 8). And so the familiarity of Ubayy with the Qur'an in this way allowed him to attain to such a bounty, honour and dignity that is only possible for a very few select people other than the prophets; it made him subject to divine compliment. What a great honour, what great happiness…

❂

As with all other matters, the Companions followed in the footsteps of Allah's Messenger when it came to living their lives as living Qur'ans by internalising their devotion to the Qur'an and its contents. Kinana al Adawi narrates:

"One time Omar bin Khattab wrote to his army commanders:

"Identify those individuals who have memorised the Qur'an and let me know so that I may honour them and favour them and dispatch them so that they can teach the Qur'an to people".

Abu Musa al Ashari informed Omar of the more than 300 *hafiz's* that were under his command. A portion of the advice from the letter that Omar wrote addressing them is as follows:

"Know that the Qur'an is a treasure of honour and reward for you. Abide by it and do not try to make it conform to you. Whoever tries to make the Qur'an conform to themselves will make them fall headfirst and straight into the fire.   Whoever abides by the Qur'an, we be allowed in the Paradise of *Firdaws*. If you can, try to make the Qur'an an intercessor for you and do not let it become your enemy. Because the one that the Qur'an intercedes for will go to Paradise while the one it complains about will go to Hell. Know that the Qur'an is a source of guidance and the most enlightened of knowledge. It is the last book that has come from The Merciful. With it blind eyes, deaf ears and closed hearts are opened... (Ali al Muttaki, II, 285-6/4019).

Whenever the bright and devoted servant of Allah's Messenger, Anas bin Malik ﷺ would complete a reading of the Qur'an, he would gather his family together and read the *hatim* prayer (the prayer that is read on completion of the Qur'an). (Ibn-I Abi Shayba, al Musannaf (Hut), Riyadh, 1409, VI, 128).

From time to time Omar bin Khattab would say to Abu Musa al Ashari, who had a very beautiful voice and would read the Qur'an in a most perfect fashion:

"O Abu Musa! Come, remind us of our Lord!"

Abu Musa would then read from the Qur'an.

One time he said to Abu Musa al Ashari:

"My brother! Increase our zeal for our Lord"

And he began to read from the Qur'an. After he had read for a while, they called Omar to the prayer. The Caliph, who had been listening to the Qur'an with deep reverence, suddenly came to and asked:

"Were we not in prayer just now?" (Ibn-I Sa'd, IV, 109).

Nafi, Abdullah bin Omar's freed slave, was once asked:

"What did Abdullah used to do in his house?"

Nafi answered:

"People cannot do what he did. He would take a fresh ablution at the time for each prayer and he would open up and continually read the Qur'an between these two times". (Ibn-I Sa'd, IV, 170).

❀

Those true Memorisers of the Qur'an who become one with it attain to many divine favours both in this world and in the next. One of the friends of Allah, Mahmud Sami Ramazanoglu ﷺ has informed us about the corpse of a Hafiz that he personally saw. This hafiz had died 30 years ago previously in Adana. His grave needed to be opened and transferred to another place due to a road that was to be built. When the grave was opened he saw the corpse intact, and its white shroud still gleaming.

It has been stated in a hadith:

"*Whenever a Hamil-I Qur'an (a Memoriser of the Qur'an who has lived by its rulings, and taken on its character, and perfected himself with its wisdom) passes away, Allah commands the earth not to eat away his body. And the earth says in reply:*

"*O my Lord! How can I eat away at his body when he carries within his breast Your words?...*" (Daylami, I, 284/1112; ali al- Muttaki, I, 555/2488).

❀

We need to take the utmost care and sensitivity in our manners and respect for the Holy Qur'an which are the words of our Lord. This is because we are living at a time when we are most in need of the virtue and spirituality of the Qur'an.

For instance we should not read the Qur'an nor should we have it read without having taken our ablutions. The following verse openly and clearly states:

"No one may touch it except the purified" (Waqia) 56:79)

This verse indicates the minor ablution, the major ablution and menstruation and post-childbirth for women. The four ortho-dox schools of thought have all agreed that it is forbidden to touch the (script) of the Qur'an without being in a state of ritual purity (ablution). (Mavsuatu'l Fikhiyye, XVIII, 322).

At any rate this ruling has been applied for 1400 years since the time of the Blessed Prophet. It has been stated in a *hadith*:

"Neither the menstruating woman nor a person in a state of major ritual impurity can read from the Qur'an" (Tirmidhi, Taharah, 98/131).

"Let none other than the pure ones touch the Qur'an" (Hakim, I, 553/1447).

In addition, when the Messenger of Allah ﷺ sent Amr bin Hazm to Yemen he wrote a declaration that explained the *fard* (obligatory acts), *sunnah* (traditions of the Prophet) and the legal rulings. In that declaration Amr was told to teach the Qur'an to the people and in addition to preaching its commands and its wis-dom he was told to also prevent people from touching the Qur'an if they were not clean. (Muwatta, Qur'an, I; Kattani, 216).

Imam Malik states:

"The one who is ritually impure cannot carry the script even within a cover or upon a cushion for this is a disliked act… This is due to respect for and exaltation of the Qur'an. (Muwatta, Qur'an, 1).

Moreover, one must be careful in all matters of showing respect and reverence for it including refraining from carrying the

Qur'an below the waist, from extending one's feet out towards it, from putting any other book or any other item upon it, and from going into the toilet with it. This must be done with fervour of worship and this sensitivity should be passed on to new generations. Because the Holy Qur'an is the most important of the signs of Islam. The Holy Qur'an states:

$$\text{وَمَن يُعَظِّمْ شَعَائِرَ اللّٰهِ فَإِنَّهَا مِنْ تَقْوَى الْقُلُوبِ}$$

"As for those who honour Allah's sacred rites, that comes from the taqwa in their hearts"(Hajj 22:32)

In short, the Qur'an is a divine book sent in order for mankind to find the right path, to learn the matters that would be impossible to learn on his own, and to attain to the hereafter. In that case, to embrace it and adopt it is the smartest path to take.

The virtue of becoming one with the Qur'an is explained in a hadith as follows:

"The Qur'an is like a strong rope, one end of which is with Allah and the other end which is in your hands. Hold onto it tightly. Then you will not stray nor will you be destroyed". (Haysami, IX, 164).

The more spirituality and prosperity we obtain from the Qur'an the more we will increase in our faith. Those who lose themselves in the Qur'an by gaining the pleasure of Allah and His Messenger, are subject to divine bounties which are beyond comprehension. **May Almighty Allah bestow such bounties upon us all and facilitate this state for each of us. Amen!...**

8. *Zikrullah*[64] *and Salawat-i Sharifa*[65]

The Arabic word for the human being, *'insan'*, is thought by some to come from the same root word as *'nisyan'* which means 'to forget'. *'Nisyan'*, which is the opposite of *'zikr'* (remembrance) implies forgetfulness which is one of the greatest weaknesses of mankind. In order to make up for the harm caused by this *'nisyan'*, which is part of human nature, he needs *zikr* in order to keep *'Allah'* and his perception of himself as 'the servant', constantly active and aware in mind. Because repetition strengthens the comprehension and understanding of the thing that is repeated.

The word *'zikr'* occurs more than 250 times in the Qur'an, which indicates its particular importance in the duty of the servant. The servant needs to be a slave to Almighty Allah in the true sense of the word and reach the degree of *'marifetullah'* (knowledge of Allah). But this will only occur to the degree of the depth of the rank and feelings that the heart gains through remembrance. This is why our Sustainer has said:

"Remember your Lord in yourself humbly and fearfully, without loudness of voice, morning and evening. Do not be one of the unaware" (A'raf 7:205)

---

64. *Zikrullah* is the invocation of God. To perform zikr is to both remember Allah and to praise Him by mentioning His name and other certain words or formulas. (translators note)

65. Salawat-I sharifa is the name given to the benediction that is said after the Prophet Muhammad"s name is mentioned. It is to send blessings upon the Prophet which takes the form of many different prayers, the most common formula being "saw" which is abbreviated to saw throughout this book. (translators note)

"And remembrance of Allah is indeed the greatest good" (Ankabut 29:45)

"For people with intelligence; those who remember Allah, standing, sitting and lying on their sides..." (Al'i imran 3:191)

Once the heart, which is the ruler of the body, has come back to life through remembrance of Allah, and become enlightened enough to distinguish between truth and falsehood, it becomes like a compass guiding the body to the truth and to goodness. It gives appropriate directions to all of the members of the body that are under its command. In the end it reaches a state of servant hood with which Allah is most pleased.

Allah's Messenger ﷺ explains the virtues of remembrance of Allah as follows:

"The comparison of the one who remembers Allah with the one who does not, is like the difference between the living and the dead" (Bukhari, Dawat, 66)

Likewise those people who are far from the remembrance of Allah are also far from being the recipients of Allah's love and are thus under divine threat. The Holy Qur'an says:

"You who have faith! Do not let your wealth or children divert you from the remembrance of Allah. Whoever behaves thus, they are the losers" (Munafikun 63:9)

"...Woe to those whose hearts are hardened against the remembrance of Allah... (az Zumar, 39:22)

If someone shuts his eyes to the remembrance of the All-Merciful, We assign him a shaytan   who becomes his bosom friend " (az- zuhruf, 43:36)

"But if anyone turns away from My reminder, his life will be a dark and narrow one and on the Day of Rising We will gather him blind". (Taha, 20:24)

Because of the grave danger of remaining heedless of performing *zikrullah* (the remembrance of Allah) Almighty Allah has repeatedly warned his slaves about this matter. In one of these warnings He says:

"Is it not time that the hearts of all who have attained to faith should feel humble at the remembrance of Allah and at the truth He has sent down" (Hadid 57:16)

This verse was revealed as a warning to certain of the Companions who, having lived a painful and distressing life in Mecca, began to slacken once they had attained to bountiful provision and favour after the migration to Madina. (See Suyuti, Lubab, II, 151-52).

Even though Moses and Aaron (upon them be peace) were both prophets, Almighty Allah yet warned them when he sent them to preach to the Pharaoh as follows:

"Go, you and your brother, with My Signs and do not slacken in remembering Me" (Taha 20:42)

In this way by warning even these prophets of not distancing themselves from doing *zikr,* He willed them to be a lesson and an example (for mankind).

In speaking of the necessity of always being in a state of *zikrullah* and *murakaba* (vigilance), Allah's Messenger ﷺ said:

"*Do not delve into unnecessary talk and forget Allah. Because excessive talk that is done forgetting Allah, hardens the heart. And the one who is the furthest from Allah is the one with a hard heart*". (Tirmidhi, Zuhd, 62/2411).

The way that the hearts of the believers reach a state of sensitivity that will allow them to be free of the hardness of heedlessness and gain the pleasure of Allah passes through continual remembrance. This is not however a temporary period or a phase; this is for a lifetime, and is only possible by being conscious of *zikrullah* in every breath taken, for it is only in this way that spiritual awakening can come about.

The Prophet's wife, Aisha has said:

"Every state of the Messenger of Allah was a state of remembrance of Allah". (Muslim, Hayz, 117).

Ibn-I Abbas, said the following about the verse:

"O you who have faith! Remember Allah with unceasing remembrance" (Ahzab, 33:41)

"Allah Most High has determined a limit for every act of worship that He has made obligatory for His slaves. He has accepted the excuse of those who are exempt (for whatever reason). The exception is *zikr*. Allah Most High has not set a limit that one can reach when it comes to *zikr*. He does not accept the excuse of anybody who abandons remembering Allah, except for the one whose mind has become disturbed. Almighty Allah has commanded all people to be in a state of *zikr* under all circumstances. (Taberi, Jamiu'l Beyan an Te'vili Ayi'l Qur'an, Beirut, 1995, XXII, 22; Kurtubi, XIV, 197).

In order to encourage the performance of *zikr* and being with the people of *zikr* the Prophet Muhammad has said:

"*To sit from the morning prayer until the sun rises with a group of people that remember Allah, is more pleasing to me than rescuing four slaves from the tribe of the sons of Ishmael. Likewise to sit with a group of people who remember Allah from the time of the after-*

noon prayer until the sun sets, is more pleasing to me that freeing four people". (Abu Dawud, Ilim, 13/3667).

In addition, the benedictions that we utter for the Prophet are among the statements of *zikr*. Almighty Allah states:

"Allah and His angels call down blessings on the Prophet. O you who have faith! Call down blessings on him and ask for complete peace and safety for him" (Ahzab, 33:56).

The Prophet explained the worth of these benedictions as follows:

"Whoever sends peace and blessings upon me once, Allah Most High has mercy on him ten times over[66], wiping away ten of his mistakes and raising his rank ten degrees" (Nasai, Sahv, 55)

"Those people who will be the closest to me on the Day of Judgement are those who send much blessings and peace upon me" (Tirmidhi, Vitir, 21/484)

In addition, acts of worship such as performing the prescribed prayer, *tasbih* (glorification), *tahmid* (praise), *takbir* (exaltation) , *tahlil* (pronouncing the oneness of Allah) and *istigfar* (seeking forgiveness), and in particular reading the Qur'an and reflecting on its verses, are also considered *zikr*.

Scenes of Virtue

The Prophet's wife, Aisha informs us that when the Messenger of Allah woke up at night for worship he would pray and supplicate by reciting 10 times each *"Allahu akbar"* (Allah is the Greatest), *"Alhamdulillah"* (Praise be to Allah), *"Subhanallahi wa bihamdih"* (Glory be to Allah and praise belongs to Him), *"Subhana'l maliki'l quddus"* (Glory be to Allah, The King and Holy

66. Muslim, Salat, 70

One) "*Astagfirullah*" (I ask Allah for forgiveness), "*La ilaha illallah*" (there is no god but Allah) and then he would say ten times:

اَللّٰهُمَّ إِنِّى أَعُوذُ بِكَ مِنْ ضَيقِ الدُّنْيَا وَ ضَيقِ يَومِ القِيَامَ

"O Allah! I seek refuge in You from the distress and narrowing of this world and the hereafter"

The Prophet would then begin his salat". (Abu Dawud, Adab, 101/5085).

❁

The Messenger of Allah ﷺ would prefer *zikr* and prayers that were concise but deep in meaning. One day the Prophet's wife, Juwayriya ﵂ prayed the early dawn prayer and then sat in the spot where she prayed. The Prophet ﷺ left the house early and when he returned later that morning he found Juwayriya still sitting where he had left her.

"Have you been sitting here doing *zikr* since the time I left you?" he asked her. When she replied yes, the Prophet ﷺ said:

"If the four statements that I said three times each after parting from you were weighed against all of the zikr *that you have said since morning you will find that they are equal in terms of reward*:

سُبْحَانَ اللّٰهِ وَبِحَمْدِهِ عَدَدَ خَلْقِهِ وَرِضَا نَفْسِهِ وَزِنَةَ عَرْشِهِ وَمِدَادَ كَلِمَاتِهِ

"I absolve Allah from all defects that do not suit His station of divinity and I praise Him to the number of creatures, and till He is pleased, to the weight of the earth and to the number of words that never run out" (Muslim, Zikr, 79).

❁

The Messenger of Allah ﷺ has said:

"There are two statements that are light on the tongue, but heavy when weighed on the scales and that are pleasing to Allah, the Merciful:

سُبْحَانَ اللّٰهِ وَبِحَمْدِهِ سُبْحَانَ اللّٰهِ العَظِيمِ

"I absolve Allah of all attributes that do not suit His position of divinity and I praise Him. I again absolve Allah, the Great One, of all attributes that do not suit His station of divinity" (Bukhari, Dawat 65, Ayman, 19, Tawheed 58; Muslim, Zikr, 31).

Almighty Allah desires that the heart of His slave is together with Him at every moment. In the following verse, these people are described as being **"those who remember Allah, standing, sitting and lying on their sides,** (Al'i Imran, 3:191)...

The above *hadiths* express the virtue of this *tasbihat* (prayer of glorification) that is carried out and the greatness of its reward. That is, in one aspect it is for encouragement and persuasion. However, we should not limit the remembrance of Allah to this *tasbihat* but we should be in a continual state of *zikr*. This is essential as is required by the Qur'an and the *hadith*.

Abdullah bin Busr ﷺ narrates:

"Two Bedouins came to the Messenger of Allah to ask him a question. One of them asked:

"O Messenger of Allah! Who is the best of people?" The Messenger of Allah replied:

"The one who has a long life and whose deeds are righteous". The other asked:

"O Messenger of Allah! The rulings of Islam have increased become numerous. Tell me one deed that I can adhere to".

"Let your tongue be ever moist with the remembrance of Allah" (Ahmad, IV, 188).

As the Prophet said to be in a continual state of *zikr* is protection against heedlessness and forgetfulness for the believer. It is a means of increasing one's obedience and submission to the commands and prohibitions of Allah. That is *zikr* is also a means of prosperity and spiritual reinforcement that increases the believers enthusiasm for the religious rulings.

❀

One Companion came to the Messenger of Allah and asked:

"Which *jihad* has the greatest reward?" The Prophet replied:

"The jihad of the one who remembers Allah much". The man then asked:

"Which fast has the greatest reward?". The Prophet replied:

"The fast of the one who remembers Allah the most".

After that the man asked the same question about the one who prays, who gives almsgiving, who goes for the pilgrimage and who gives charity. The answer was the same for each of these:

"The one who remembers Allah most".

Upon this Abu Bakr ﷺ said to Omar ﷺ:

"O Omar! Those who remember Allah have taken the entire share of goodness". The Prophet ﷺ then turned towards them and said:

"Yes, that is true". (Ahmad, III, 438; Haysami, X, 74).

In all cases then, we will profit greatly if we train ourselves to be in a constant of *zikr*.

❀

Muadh bin Jabal ﷺ narrates:

"I once said to the Prophet 🌸:

"O Messenger of Allah! Give me some advice"

The Messenger of Allah 🌸 replied:

"Have fear of Allah to the best of your ability. Remember Allah wherever you are, next to a stone or a tree. And for the sin that you have done in secret, seek forgiveness in secret, but for the one you have done openly, seek forgiveness openly. (Haysami, X, 74).

❁

One day the Messenger of Allah 🌸 was telling his companions about the virtue of gatherings of *zikr*:

"*When you come to the gardens of Paradise make sure to benefit from them properly*"

"What do you mean by the gardens of Paradise o Messenger of Allah" they asked him.

The Prophet replied:

"*The gatherings of zikr*" (Tirmidhi, Deavat, 82/3510).

❁

Whenever Abdullah bin Rawaha 🌸 came across one of the Companions he would say:

"Come my brother! Let us sit for a while for Allah and refresh our faith in our Sustainer (Let us do zikr)".

One Companion who did not understand what this meant went to the Prophet and informed him of the situation. The Prophet said to him:

"*May Allah have mercy on Abdullah bin Rawaaha. He loves the chains of zikr which the angels praise*" (Ahmad, III, 265).

❁

Abdullah bin Shaddad 🕮 narrates:

"Three people from the tribe of Bani Uzra came to the Messenger of Allah 🕮 and became Muslim. The Messenger of Allah asked:

"Who will undertake the care of these?

Talha 🕮 said:

"I will o Messenger of Allah".

While they were with Talha, the Messenger of Allah 🕮 dispatched a small troop of soldiers. One of the three of these people came out of this unit and was martyred. Then he sent another small troop. From this the second person came out, but was also martyred. The third person died in his bed a little while later.

Talha narrates:

"I saw these three people who were staying with me in Paradise. The one who died in his bed was foremost, then the second martyr, then last came the person who was martyred first of all. I was surprised and a little upset at this situation. I immediately told the Prophet of Allah what I saw. He said:

"This is nothing to be surprised about. There is no one in the eyes of Allah who is of more virtue than the believer who constantly performs glorification of Allah, takbir, and tahlil and who lives his life based on Islam. (Ahmad, I, 163).

One day Uftade went out to the countryside with his students for a talk. Following orders, all of the derwishes walked around the most beautiful parts of the countryside and brought a bunch of flowers for their teacher. However in the hands of the old Judge of Bursa, Mahmud Efendi, who would later find fame as Aziz Mahmud Hudayi, brought back a withered flower whose stem had been broken... After the others presented their flowers to their teacher with happiness, Mahmud Efendi, presented his broken and withered flower to Uftade his head bowed down. Amongst the curious looks of the other students, Uftade asked:

"Mahmud my son! Why, when everyone brought bouquets and bouquets of flowers, did you bring a withered broken flower?"

With great modesty of manners, Mahmud Efendi bowed his head and answered:

"Master! Whatever I present you would never be enough. But whichever flower I bent down to pick I found it in a state of remembrance of its Lord, and saying '*Allah, Allah*'. My heart couldn't bear to hinder this remembrance of theirs. Helpless I was compelled to bring this flower which was unable to continue its *zikr*".

For those with a soft heart, every atom in the universe consists of lessons to take heed from. All things, whether they be living or non-living perform zikr of Allah. It is stated in Quranic verse:

"The seven heavens and the earth and everyone in them glorify Him. There is nothing which does not glorify Him with praise but you do not understand their glorification. He is All-Forbearing, Ever-Forgiving.(Isra, 17:44).

And so man must be conscious of his true duty by taking heed from this magnificent scene in the universe and should not remain heedless of remembering his Lord.

The mos*t* virtuous of our *zikr* is

salawat – i sharif. A believer will benefit spiritually to the degree that he sends peace and blessings upon the Messenger of Allah ﷺ. This is because the value of our Prophet in the eyes of Allah is most high.

Firstly our Lord personally performs prayers on the Messenger of Allah ﷺ and has raised him in degree through his mercy and pleasure and has bestowed upon him mercy.

One of the times when we send blessings upon the Prophet ﷺ is during the prayer, when we read the *Tahiyyat* prayer[67]. According to what has been transmitted, the Prophet said:

"On the night of the Ascension, I saw our Lord with the eye of my heart. Allah Most High said to me:

"Speak to me o beloved!"

I was frozen in my astonishment. Then Allah Most High inspired my heart to say the following words:

اَلتَّحِيَّاتُ لِلّٰهِ وَالصَّلَوَاتُ وَالطِّيِّبَاتُ

"All of worship, be it verbal like praise, active like prayer and fasting or financial such as the alms-giving, is particular to Allah – Most Glorious and Exalted".

Upon this Allah Most High said:

لَسَّلَامُ عَلَيْكَ أَيُّهَا النَّبِىُّ وَرَحْمَةُ اللّٰهِ وَبَرَكَاتُهُ

"O Most Honoured Prophet! May the peace, mercy and bless-ings of Allah be upon you".

In response I said:

---

67. This is the prayer that is said whilst in the sitting position of salat (translator's note)

اَلسَّلَامُ عَلَيْنَا وَ عَلَى عِبَادِ اللهِ الصَّالِحِينَ

"May the peace of Allah be upon us and upon all of Allah's righteous slaves".

Allah Most High then said:

"O My Prophet! I removed even Gabriel from between us. You have not removed your community from amongst us".

Hearing these words intended to be humorous, Almighty Allah, Gabriel said:

أَشْهَدُ أَنْ لَا إِلَهَ إِلَّا اللهُ وَأَشْهَدُ أَنَّ مُحَمَّدًا عَبْدُهُ وَرَسُولُهُ

"I bear witness that there is no god who is worthy of worship other than Allah. And I also bear witness that Muhammad the Trustworthy is His slave and Messenger" (See Qurtubi, III, 425).

❋

Ubayy bin Ka'b ﷺ narrates:

"One time when one third of the night had passed, the Messenger of Allah awoke and rose and said:

"O people! Remember Allah! Remember Allah! The first trumpet will be blown and will upheave the earth from one place to another. Then the next trumpet will be blown. Death will come and strike in all of its intensity. Death will come and strike in all of its intensity".

I asked the Prophet:

"O Messenger of Allah! I send abundant blessings and peace upon you, but I wonder, should I do more? [how much is enough]?"

"Do as much as you wish", he said.

"If I allot a fourth of my prayer to sending blessings and peace upon you, would that be sufficient?" I asked.

"*Allot as much as you wish. But if you do more, that will be better for you*" he said.

"In that case I will assign half of my supplication to sending blessings and peace upon you" I said.

"*Do as much as you wish. But if you do more, than that will be better for you*".

"In that case will two-thirds be enough?" I asked.

"*As much as you like. But if you increase, it will be much better for you*" he said.

When I said:

"In that case what if I assign all of my supplication to sending peace and blessings upon you?", he replied:

"*In that case Allah will remove all your distress and forgive you your sins*". (Tirmidhi, Qiyamah, 23/2457).

One time when the Blessed Prophet ﷺ saw one of his Companions begin his supplication by praising Allah and sending blessings upon the Prophet, he praised him and said:

"*O you who performs the prayer! Supplicate (as long as you begin your supplication with praise and prayers upon me), and your prayers will be answered*" (Tirmidhi Dawat, 64, 3476).

Omar bin Khattab ﷺ said:

"(On its own), the supplication you make stands between the heavens and the earth. If you do not send blessings upon the Prophet, not one of your prayers will rise to Allah" (Tirmidhi, witr, 21/486).

Ka'b bin Ujra narrates that one day we said to the Messenger of Allah:

"O Messenger of Allah! We have learned how to send peace upon you, but we don't know how to send blessings upon you". He responded:

Say these words:

اَللّٰهُمَّ صَلِّ عَلَى مُحَمَّدٍ وَعَلَى آلِ مُحَمَّدٍ كَمَا صَلَّيْتَ عَلَى (إِبْرَاهِيمَ وَعَلَى)

آلِ إِبْرَاهِيمَ إِنَّكَ حَمِيدٌ مَجِيدٌ اَللّٰهُمَّ بَارِكْ عَلَى مُحَمَّدٍ وَعَلَى آلِ مُحَمَّدٍ كَمَا

بَارَكْتَ عَلَى (إِبْرَاهِيمَ وَعَلَى) آلِ إِبْرَاهِيمَ إِنَّكَ حَمِيدٌ مَجِيدٌ

"O Allah! Have mercy on Muhammad and his family just as you had mercy on Abrahim and his family. Truly You are worthy of praise and most exalted. O Allah! Bestow goodness and bounty on Muhammad and on the family of Muhammad just as you bestowed goodness and bounty on Abraham and on the family of Abraham. Truly You are worthy of praise and most exalted". (Bukhari, Deawat, 32, Tirmidhi, Witr, 20; Ibn-I Majah, Iqama, 25).

The Messenger of Allah said:

"The most virtuous of your days is Friday... For this reason, you should send much blessings and peace on me on this day, the day when they will be presented to me".

Upon this the Companions asked:

"O Messenger of Allah! How can our *salat-u salam* be presented to you once you have passed away and there is no trace of you". The Prophet replied:

"Allah Most High has forbidden the earth to decompose the bodies of the prophets". (Abu Dawud, Salat 201/1047, Witr, 26)

✳

Ali ﷻ has the following to say about the virtue of sending peace and blessings on the Prophet on a Friday:

"Whoever sends one hundred blessings on the Prophet on a Friday, will appear at the gathering on the Day of Judgement with a beautiful and radiant face. The people will ask each other longingly: "I wonder which deed this man used to perform". (Bayhaki, ShuAbu'l Imam, III 212)

✳

Ka'b bin Ujra ﷻ narrates:

"One day the Messenger of Allah ﷺ told us to approach the pulpit. We did so. He climbed the first step, then said "amen". He climbed the second step and said "amen". He climbed the third step in the same way, saying "amen".

When he had come down from the pulpit we asked:

"O Messenger of Allah! We have heard some things from you today that we have never heard before. (What is the wisdom in this").

He replied:

"Gabriel came to me and said: Let the one who reaches the month of Ramadan without having his sins forgiven be far from mercy". I said "amen". When I had climbed the second stair, he said:

"Let the one who hears Your name but does not send blessings upon You be far from mercy". I said "Amen". When I had climbed the third step he said:

"Let the one who has not been able to gain Paradise because his mother or father, or both have reached old-age beside him but he

217

has not been able to please them. And I said: amen". (Hakim, IV, 170/7256; Tirmidhi, Deawat, 100/3545).

❋

It has been reported by a righteous individual:

"I once had a neighbour who used to make copies of the books of scholars by writing them out himself. When he died I saw him in my dream. I asked him:

"How did Allah Most High treat you". He said:

"He has forgiven me".

"Which deed of yours was the means for this" I asked.

"Whenever I used to write the blessed and honourable name of the Messenger of Allah ﷺ in a book I would never fail to send blessings and peace upon him. And so my Lord has bestowed upon me favours that no eye has ever seen, no ear has heard of, and no person has ever been able to imagine". (Nebhani, Saadet'ul Dareyn, pg 101).

❋

It has been narrated that an individual who had failed to adopt the character of the Prophet ﷺ saw him in his dream one night. The Messenger of Allah ignored him. Sadly he asked:

"O Messenger of Allah! Are you upset with me?"

"No".

"In that case why are you ignoring me?"

"I don't know who you are".

"How can that be o Messenger of Allah! I am from your community. The scholars say that you can recognise members of your community better than a mother recognises her own child..."

"That is true. However, I do not see any trace of my character on you. In addition, no blessings or peace have ever come to me from you. Know that I only recognise those of my community to the degree that they have taken on my character".

On awakening from his sleep deeply saddened, this believer then repented for his former state and took on the praiseworthy character of the Prophet. He spent a great portion of his time sending peace and blessings on the Prophet. A little while later he saw the Messenger of Allah in his dream once more. This time the Messenger of Allah said to him:

"Now I know you and I will intercede for you"…

In short, the Prophet ﷺ has said:

"A person will be together with the one he loves". (Bukhari, Adab, 96). According to the principle 'the lover loves everything about their beloved', we must follow the Prophet ﷺ in all our actions and states. It is such that the love and ardour in this matter is like the backbone of love of Allah. All love contrary to this love has been invalidated by the way of the Qur'an and the *Sunnah.*

The only way to reach Almighty Allah, that is to be reunited with Him is achieved by love of His Beloved Prophet.

Zikrullah and *salawat-I sharif* are nourishment for our spiritual existence and assurance for our eternal happiness. The worlds of our heart and soul find completion with *zikr* (remembrance of Allah). Almighty Allah has said:

"Only in the remembrance of Allah can the heart find peace". (Ar Rad, 13:28).

The way to being a servant who is dear to Allah passes through continual zikr (remembrance). It is only through this way that our lives can gain spiritual pleasure and sweetness. May Allah let us all partake of it. Amen…

9. Anxiety and preparation for death and the afterlife

When a person looks at the order of the universe with the eye of discernment he realises that the issue that he should be most concerned with is the fact of death.

Almighty Allahhas said:

"Everyone on it will pass away". (Ar Rahman, 55:26).

"Every self shall taste death". (Anbiya, 21:35).

How strange it is that people – visitors in this world for two or three days – (yet) delude themselves. Though they watch scenes of death every day, yet do they see death as being distant from themselves. They think they are the absolute possessors of the fleeting trust which it is possible they will lose at every instant. Whereas every person, on entering this world, has his soul clothed in a body and is destined to travel the path to death. He has entered the preparatory realm for that path but he fails to remember this. Then the day arrives when his spirit is separated from his body. In the grave, which is the door to the hereafter, he is farewelled to another great journey. Allah Most High says:

"When We grant long life to people, We return them to their primal state. So will you not use your intellect? (Do they not perceive this journey and take heed from it". (Yasin, 36:68).

The principle aim of this worldly life for mankind is to live a life of servant hood that Allah is pleased with and to thereby gain eternal happiness. The Messenger of Allah has said:

"The intelligent person is the one who does not yield to the desires and whims of their nafs and who prepares for what is to come after death..." (Tirmidhi, Qiyamah, 25/2459).

How beautifully the late Najip Fazil expressed this:

"O niggardly (merchant), sew yourself a different money-bag".

And save up whatever currency is valid in the grave!"...

Life is like the drops that fill up a glass of water. The clarity of the glass depends on how clear the drops are. The last drop to fill the glass is the person's last breath.

It is stated in a hadith:

"Whoever's last words in life are 'La ilaha illallah' will enter Paradise". (Abu Dawud, Janaiz, 15-16/3116; Hakim, I, 503).

That is, the one who eliminates unnecessary whims, pleasures and carnal desires from their heart and fills it with love of Allah and continues in this way living a spiritual life until their last moment, will, it is hoped, migrate from this world with faith and enter Paradise. Because it is very difficult for a person who leads a different life to say *'la ilaha illallah'* at the last breath. The Messenger of Allah ﷺ said:

"A person dies as they live and will be raised up as they died". (See Muslim, Jannah, 83; Munawi, V, 663).

A person's last breath is like a clear mirror, free of mist. A person will know themselves most accurately at their last breath. The account of their life will be displayed before their heart and their eyes. This is why there is no scene more cautionary than the point of death.

The Prophet ﷺ said:

"According to one's deeds, the grave is either a garden from the gardens of Paradise or a pit from the pits of hell". (Tirmidhi, Qiyamah, 26/2460).

Thus it is vital that we prepare well our numbered breaths for the last breath that we will take if we want to leave this mortal world as a good slave and to make our grave a garden from the gardens of Paradise. A prosperous and guided worldly life, embellished with righteous deeds, is a must for a happy afterlife.

Almighty Allah has said:

"And worship your Lord until what is Certain comes to you". (Hijr, 15:99).

Those special slaves who live their lives in this way, with love for Allah and His Messenger and who adorns them with righteous deeds – through the grace of Allah- will migrate with the spiritual peace of the 'statement of witnessing'[68] in their last moments. In contrast, those unfortunate ones who are deceived by the fleeting, relative and carnal attractions on this earth and who weaken their spiritual characteristics will, in the majority of cases, die according to how they lived their lives and will be subject to loss and abasement and contempt under the earth.

The Messenger of Allah ﷺ said as a warning to his community:

"There is nobody who will die and not feel regret".

"What is that regret o Messenger of Allah" he was asked.

The Prophet replied:

"If the one who dies is a good person (a possessor of goodness and righteousness) then he will regret not increasing this state of his;

---

68. The statement of witnessing is as follows: I bear witness that there is no Allahbut Allah and that Muhammad is hte Messenger of Allah (translator's note)

if the person is bad, he will regret not giving up his evil and reform-ing himself". (Tirmidhi, Zuhd, 59/2403).

Almighty Allah warns his slaves in this matter:

"O you who have faith! Do not let your wealth or children divert you from the remembrance of Allah. Whoever does that is lost. Give from what We have provided for you before death comes to one of you and he says, "My Lord, if only you would give me a little more time so that I can give charity and be one of the righteous people!" Allah will not give anyone more time, once their time has come. Allah is aware of what you do" (Munafiquun, verses 9-11)

In short, our death and our lives in the grave which will con-tinue until the Day of Judgement will take shape according to the state of our worldly life and our deeds.

How beautifully Jaluluddin Al Rumi has expressed it:

"My son, each person's death is the colour of their own self. For those who abhor death and who are enemies to it, not realis-ing that it is a reunion with Allah, death appears like a frightening enemy. For those who are friends with death, it appears as a friend.

O soul that fears and flees from death! If you want the truth of the matter it is not death that you fear, but rather your own self.

Because what it is that you see and thus fear and shiver about in the mirror of death is not the appearance of death but your own ugly appearance. Your spirit is like a tree. And death is like the leaves of the tree. Each leaf is according to the type of tree (it is on)…"

Thus death becomes attractive depending on how much one beautifies one's life with righteous deeds.

Scenes of Virtue

Abdullah bin Omar ﷺ narrates: "I was once with the Messenger of Allah ﷺ. A man from the *Ansar* came to Allah's Messenger, greeted him and asked:

"O Messenger of Allah! Who is the most virtuous of the believers?" The Prophet replied:

"*The one who has the best character*". This time the man asked:

"Well, who is the most intelligent of the believers?" The Prophet replied:

"*The one who remembers death the most and who prepares for what's to come after it in the best way. That is true intelligence*". (Ibn-I Majah, Zuhd, 31).

❀

Bara ﷺ narrates:

"We were once with the Messenger of Allah ﷺ at a funeral prayer. The Prophet ﷺ sat next to the grave and began to cry such that the earth around him became wet with his tears. Then he said:

"*O my brothers! Prepare well for death (which is to befall us all)*". (Ibni Majah, Zuhd, 19).

❀

Omar ﷺ ordered one of his servants to repeat the following sentence to him everyday:

"O Omar! Do not forget death". However when some white hairs appeared in his beard he said to his servant:

"That will do. My white beard is now a reminder of death for me at every instant".

In truth we must not forget our mortality. We must remember death in order to control the desires of our soul.

❂

The Prophet Muhammad ﷺ has informed us of certain scenes from the grave, the Day of Judgement and the afterlife in order for us to reflect and take heed and to prepare for our last breath, for death, and for what's to come after death. Some of these are described below:

"When a Muslim enters the throes of death, the angels of mercy appear before him with a silk white dress and say:

"Exit from your body, pleased with your Lord and your Lord pleased with you. Reunite with the mercy of Allah and the sweetest of scents and your Lord who has no anger towards you".

The spirit then leaves the body accompanied by the most beautiful of musk scents. The angels hand him back and forth until they bring him to the gates of heaven and it is said:

"How beautiful is this smell that has come with you from the earth". Then they take him to the other believing spirits. These believing spirits are more pleased with his coming than one of you would be if he found something that he had lost. They ask him:

"What happened to so and so? What happened to so and so?" That is, they ask about those left behind in the world. Some of the spirits answer (about one of those who has been asked about):

"Leave him alone. He has buried himself in the anxiety of the world". Then the newly arrived spirit asks:

"So and so died. Did not he come to you?" They answer:

"Is that so? In that case, he has gone where he was supposed to, he has been taken to the Fire.

When a non-believer enters the throes of death, the angels of punishment appear with an ugly dress made of fine bristles and say:

"Leave this body, angry yourself and having drawn the wrath of Allah upon you and run to the punishment of Allah".

Then the spirit leaves with the worst of smells. The angels bring it to the gate of the earth and say:

"How bad is this smell!" Then they take him to the other unbelieving spirits". (Nasai, Jenaiz, 9).

Allah's Messenger has informed us:

"On the Day of Judgement the son of Adam will be brought like a lamb and stood before Allah and Allah Most High will say to him:

"I gave you plenty of bounty and property. I showered you with such favours and blessings. What did you do in return?" He will say:

"O my Lord, I amassed it, I increased it, I left it behind in a much greater quantity than it was. Let me go back to the world and bring it back to You".

Allah Most High will say:

"First show me what you have sent on for your afterlife". He will say again:

"O my Lord, I amassed it, I increased it, I left it behind in a much greater quantity than it was. Let me go back to the world and bring it back to You".

This is because this slave had not sent forth anything worth any good. And this is why he will be thrown into the hellfire". (Tirmidhi, Qiyamah, 6/2427).

And so those people who have wasted the life of this world in heedlessness and have not made any preparations for the hereafter will meet with a dismal end. Almighty Allah informs us of this in the Holy Qur'an:

"But as for him whose record shall be given to him behind his back He will in time pray for utter destruction. But he will enter the blazing flame. Behold [in his earthly life], he lived joyfully among people of his own kind- for, behold, he never thought he would have to return to Allah". (Inshiqaq, 84:10-14)

Another example of the grievous end of those who rely upon their worldly fortune, position, and power and become impertinent, and conceited and smug as a result is Qarun. Almighty Allah informs us of his story full of warning for us as follows:

"Qarun was one of the people of Musa but he lorded it over them. We gave him treasures, the keys alone to which were a heavy weight for a party of strong men. When his people said to him, "Do not gloat. Allah does not love people who gloat. Seek the abode of the afterlife with what Allah has given you, without forgetting your portion of the world. And do good as Allah has been good to you. And do not seek to cause corruption in the earth. Allah does not love corrupters". He said, "I have only been given it because of knowledge I have". Did he not know that before him Allah had destroyed generations with far greater strength than his and far more possessions? The evildoers will not be questioned about their sins. He went out among his people in his finery. Those who desired the life of the world said, "Oh! If only we had the same as Qarun has been given! What immense good fortune he possesses". But those who had been given knowledge said, "Woe to you! Allah's reward is better for those who have faith and act rightly. But only the steadfast will obtain it". We caused the earth to swallow up both him and his

house. There was no group to come to his aid, besides Allah, and he was not someone who is helped" (Qasas, 28:76-81)

The story of Qarun is a clear example of the end affair of those heedless people who depend on and are self-satisfied with their wealth and power in this world and who forget that one day they too will die.

❋

One day the Prophet ﷺ was asked:

"O Messenger of Allah! Will we be able to see our Lord on the Day of Judgement?" The Prophet asked them:

"Do you ever have any difficulty in seeing the sun at noon on a cloudless day?

When they replied "no" he asked them again:

"Do you need to push and shove each other when you want to see the moon on a cloudless night?"

When his companions again answered "No, O Messenger of Allah", he said:

"I swear by the One who holds my soul in His hands that there will be no pushing and shoving when it comes to seeing your Lord. Just as when you don't have to push and shove each other to see the sun and the moon. In this way the slave will come face to face with his servant. Allah Most High will ask:

"O so and so. Did I not favour you? Did I not make you lord over all creation you? Did I not give you a wife? Did I not make the horse and the camel subservient to you? Did I not make you a leader, so that you could take one-fourth of the property from booty for yourself?" The slave will answer:

"Yes O Lord!"

Allah Most High will then ask:

"So did you not think that you would ever meet me?"

The slave will answer:

"No o Lord!"

Allah Most High will then say:

"In that case now it is I who is overlooking you. Just as you forgot Me in the world".

Then a second slave appears before Allah. Allah Most High asks him the same questions. Then He asks a third slave the same questions. Each time, the slave is forced to confirm what His Lord says each time.

Allah Most High then says:

"Did it never occur to you that you would meet with Me?" The slave replies:

"O My Lord! I believed in You, and in Your books, and in Your prophets. I prayed, I fasted, I gave charity!" To the best of his ability he sings praises of Allah Most High. Allah Exalted and Majestic is He says:

"In that case stop! A witness will now come against you". The slave thinks to himself:

"Who will be a witness against me?" The slave's mouth will be sealed. His thighbone, his flesh and his bones will be told: "Come now speak up". His thighbone, flesh and bones will speak out and confess everything that the slave ever did. This is so the slave can not put up any excuses. This person is the hypocrite who has come up against the wrath of Allah". (Muslim, Zuhd, 16).

How can the slave hide his sins in a court in which all of his limbs and the earth will be a witness against him? Thus must we

229

live our lives with the utmost care and vigilance if we do not wish to be put to shame there.

✿

The Messenger of Allah ﷺ said:

"When the slave is placed in his grave and his close ones part from him – and he can hear their footsteps as they (walk away) – two angels appear before him. They sit him down and ask him:

"What did you use to think of Muhammad ﷺ?" If the person asked is a believer he replies to this question as follows:

"I bear witness that he is Allah's slave and Messenger!" They say to him:

"Look at your place in hell. Allah has transformed it into a garden from Paradise". The man looks and sees both places. Then Allah opens up a window in his grave that looks onto Paradise.

If the deceased person is an unbeliever or a hypocrite, he replies to the angels" question as follows:

"I don't know the person you are speaking of. I merely used to repeat what others were saying". It will be said to him:

"You did not understand and you did not follow". Then he will be beaten between his ears with an iron rod. He will scream with such pain (from the rod) that all creatures near him (except for man and jinn) will hear him". (Bukhari, Jenaiz, 68, 87; Muslim, Jannah, 70).

✿

The Prophet Soloman, the son of the Prophet David ﷺ once passed by a farmer who was ploughing a field. The farmer said:

"Undoubtedly the family of David has been given great dominion".

The wind transmitted these words to the ear of Soloman who immediately descended from his animal and walked towards the farmer:

"I walked over to you in order that you do not desire something that you cannot bear". Then he continued his words:

"Glorification made by a slave that is acceptable to Allah Most High is undoubtedly better than all of the property and dominion given to the family of David".

In truth, in this mortal world the good deeds that we do with sincerity will be our capital and happiness in the eternal realm. It is stated in a noble verse:

"You who have faith! Fear Allah and let each self look to what it has sent forward for Tomorrow. Fear Allah. Allah is aware of what you do". (Hashr, 59:18)

There is no way to escape death. The only way out then is to prepare for it. The Messenger of Allah ﷺ has said:

"The Prophet David عليه السلام was very passionate in his efforts in his religion and was very particular about his honour. Whenever he left the house he would make sure to close the door securely so that no one could enter until he had returned. One day he left his house and closed his door... When David returned, he saw a man sitting in the middle of his house. He said to him:

"Who are you?" The man answered:

"I am the one who fears no king, nor are any veils an obstruction for me". Hearing this, David said:

"In that case by Allah, you are the angel of death. Welcome by Allah's command".

A little while later his spirit was taken by the angel..." (Ahmad, II, 419).

This is the way that those who are always ready for death greet the Angel of Death, Azrail...

How beautifully the late Najip Fazil has expressed it:

(At that moment) in which the curtains rise and the curtains fall

The (skill) is to be able to say "Welcome Azrail".

❋

We should forward on the favours that Allah has bestowed upon us to the afterlife while we still have the chance and make preparations for the difficult and dire Day of Judgement. The following wise words of Abu Dharr ﷺ are a nice summary of the necessity and the way of preparing for death and what follows it.

"There are three shareholders in any piece of property. The first is the owner, that is, you. The second is fate. It does not ask you whether it will bring good or evil such as misfortune or death. The third is your heir. It waits impatiently for you to lay your head down as soon as possible, (that is for you to die) and it takes away your property and you have to account for it. If you are able, do not be the most powerless of these three shareholders!

Allah Most High has said: لَن تَنَالُوا الْبِرَّ حَتَّى تُنفِقُوا مِمَّا تُحِبُّونَ "You will not attain true goodness until you give of what you love". (Al'i Imran, 3: 92).

Here is my most beloved possession… this camel. In order to meet with it again in Paradise, I am sending it ahead of me (that is I am giving it away to charity)" (Abu Nuaym, Hilya, I, 163).

✤

There was once a famous scholar named Ucbas Nureddin Hamza Efendi[69] who lived during the Ottoman period. He used to save his money because he could not bear to spend it. He would not mount a horse and would make do with old clothes and shoes. In this way he would save his money. This is why he used to be known amongst the people as 'The money-loving Hodja'.

This hodja built Ucbas Madrese in Fatih Karagumruk and then later the Ucbas Masjid with the money he saved up. He had rooms made for scholars and poor people to live in and created many endowments for these. When those who knew him heard of this they were shocked and mocked him saying:

"Hodja, how could you part with your money which you love so much?"

The hodja gave the following significant and witty reply:

"My dear friends! You are right. I do love my money. This is why I couldn't bear to leave it in this world. So I have sent it on ahead of me to the afterlife".

✤

Ali ؓ has said:

"The world has turned its back and is leaving. The afterlife is ahead of us and awaits us. Each has its own children (followers).

---

69. This Hodja was given the nickname Ucbas because he was born in the village of Ucbas which is part of Karasu. He is from the scholarly class and (was a judge). He died in 948/1541. For his life and details about this particular event see Taskopruzade, As Shaiku'n Numaniyye (thk. A. Suphi Furat), pg 540-541).

Be the followers of the hereafter, not of this world. Today is the day to do good deeds, while there is no accounting. Tomorrow is the calling to account, where there is no more chance to do any good". (Bukhari, Rikak, 4).

Just like the student who leaves the examination hall can no longer answer any more of the questions or improve his grade...

Benefiting from these words of Ali, some friends of Allah have said the following:

"The world has turned its back and is leaving while the after-life is headed towards us. How amazing is the one who turns towards that which has turned its back and is leaving, and yet he himself turns his back on and pays no heed to the one coming towards him..."

Abu Dharda 🙵 used to say:

"I fear for you that you will become absorbed in the blessings that amuse man and be carried away with secret desire. This desire arises when, though you are hungry in terms of knowledge, you fill your stomachs with food. The best of you is the one who advises his friend as follows:

"Come let us fast before we die".

The worst amongst you is the one who says to his friend:

"Come let us enjoy ourselves before we die. Let us eat and drink and enjoy life to the fullest and get as much pleasure out of it as we can..." (Abu Nuaym, Hilya, I, 218).

The back of Sufyan-i Sevri became bent at a very young age. He used to say to those who asked him the reason:

"I had a teacher from whom I was learning knowledge. Even though I tried to convince him to say the testament of faith while he was dying he was not able to say it. Seeing this state bent my back".

Apart from the prophets, no one is guaranteed the state of their last breath. In fact the prophet Joseph ﷺ prayed to almighty Allah:

"… (o Allah!) … take me as a Muslim at my death and join me to the people who are righteous". (Yusuf, 12:101).

The fact that Joseph sought refuge in Allah shows that even the prophets were concerned about their last breath. This is why the believer must always struggle amongst feelings of hope and fear and must accumulate his provision for the hereafter.

❁

When Shakik-i Belhi once passed by a grave he looked at it cautiously and said to those who were with him:

"Most of these here have realised now that that this world deceived them…"

"Why" they asked him. He answered:

"Did they not think that while they were living they had property, wealth, a house, a mount, relatives, gardens and fields? But now here you see that this is not the reality…"

❁

The following state of the friend of Allah, Rabi bin Haysem ﷺ, is a striking example of how one should frequently call one's *nafs* to account in order to prepare for death and the hereafter:

Rabi bin Haysem once dug a grave in his backyard. At times when he felt that his heart had become hardened, he would enter this grave and lie there for a while. He would reflect on the fact that one day he would leave this world and be left in a position of having to seek refuge and accept charity while in the grave. Thinking that he would have to account for his actions in the hereafter, he would begin to seek forgiveness.

Then he would read the following verse:

حَتَّى إِذَا جَاءَ أَحَدَهُمُ الْمَوْتُ قَالَ رَبِّ ارْجِعُونِ لَعَلِّي أَعْمَلُ صَالِحاً فِيمَا تَرَكْتُ

"When death comes to one of them, he says, "My Lord, send me back again, so that perhaps I may act rightly regarding the things I failed to do!" (Mu'minuun, 23:99-100)

When he got out from the grave he would say to himself:

"O Rabi! Look, today you have been returned to life. There is going to be a day when this wish of yours will not be accepted and you will not be sent back to this world. Take your precautions now and increase your righteous deeds, your struggle in the path of Allah and your preparations for the hereafter…"

How beautiful is the following advice of Imam Ghazzali:

"Every day after praying the dawn prayer and before one begins the new day, each believer should come face to face with his own soul and make certain contracts with it and come to agreement about certain conditions. Just as if a merchant has to leave his capital to his partner he makes a contract with him. And he does not fail to warn him of certain things. Man too should warn and caution his soul of the following:

"My capital is my life. When my life departs from me, my capital will be lost and profit and gain will come to an end. However this day is a new day. Allah Most High has allowed me this day and has favoured me. If he had of taken my life I would certainly have hoped to be sent back for at least a day in order to be able to carry out good deeds. Now assume that your life has been taken away and you have been sent back. In that case do not commit sins or bad deeds today and do not spend even a moment of this day fruitlessly. Because each breath is a priceless blessing.

Know well that a day is 24 hours with its night and its day. On the Day of Judgement, 24 closed boxes for each day will be brought before man. When one of the boxes is brought forth and opened, the slave sees that it is full of light as a reward for his good deeds that he performed at that hour. He is so pleased thinking about the reward that Allah will bestow, that if this joy of his were to be divided amongst the people of the hellfire they would not feel the pain of (it). When the second box is opened and it is full of darkness and a disgusting stench, then this is the hour that the slave passed in rebellion. The slave will be so sad at this that if this sadness were to be divided amongst the people of Paradise they would not be able to taste the joy of it due to their sadness. A third box will be opened and this will be entirely empty. This represents the time that the slave spent in sleep or performing lawful actions. However on that day when there is an intense need for the reward from even the smallest deed, the slave will burn with regret, even more so that a merchant who has lost an enormous gain even though he had plenty of opportunity and he will cringe with pain at having spent that hour in vain.

In that case, o my evil-commanding soul! Fill your box well while you have the chance and dare not leave it empty. Do not fall into laziness or you will fall from the greatest of heights!"

❋

Halid-i Baghdadi, who reached the peak of the outer and inner sciences passed his entire life anxious at his last breath. He writes in his *Mektubat*:

"...I swear by Allah Most High that I do not believe that I have ever done a single act of goodness that is acceptable and valid in the eyes of Allah from the time my mother gave birth to me until today. (Yet do I seek refuge in the Mercy of my Lord). If you do not see your own soul as bankrupt in terms of performing all acts of good, then this is the peak of ignorance...[70]

The following extract from a letter he sent to a friend are a reflection of this anxiety of preparing for his last breath:

"...I hope that you occupy yourselves with what will be needed when you take your last breath, that you carry out acts suitable to the traditions of the Prophet, that you do not pay any attention to the deceptive beauties of this fleeting world, and that you do not forget to pray for this poor slave. Pray that he meets with success and a good end with faith in his heart having lived the way Allah wishes". (Mektubat-I Mawlana Halid, p 175).

And so the great friends of Allah never relied on their own deeds and constantly sought refuge in the mercy and forgiving nature of Allah when it came to the matter of their last breath. In that case, we too should not rely upon our knowledge or our actions and must constantly pray to Almighty Allah that we meet with a good end.

❈

At one time there was a man who used to run a store which was located at the exit gate of the city. Whenever a funeral used to pass by this gate this man would toss a seed into an urn that stood by him and at the end of the month he would count the seeds and say:

"This month, this many people fell into that urn".

---

70. Halid-I Baghdadi, Mektubat-I Mawlana Halid, Istanbul, 1993, pg 178).

And so it was that one day he too passed away. Quite a while had passed when a friend, unaware of his death came to visit him. When he couldn't see him, he asked the neighbours:

"What happened to the owner of this store?"

They said:

"He too fell into the urn"…

What lesson to take heed from…Let us not forget that every person will fall into the urn of death… However, people in general watch others around them migrate to the eternal realm one by one, yet out of their heedlessness, they see their own death as far, far away…

❈

The servant of Yavuz Sultan Selim Han, Hasan Can narrates: "Once a boil had formed on the back of Sultan Yavuz. The boil grew in a short time and became a deep cavity. It grew so much that we could see the liver of Yavuz through that cavity. He was suffering badly. He was like a wounded lion. But somehow he remained unable to accept his powerlessness and continued to give commands and directions to his soldiers. I approached him and indicating his own condition, he asked me:

"Hasan Can, what is this state?"

I sensed that his mortal journey had come to an end and that he was about to begin his eternal life. That is why I said to him sorrowfully, the pain of separation burning in my heart:

"My Sultan, I think your time has come to be with Allah Most High".

The great Sultan turned to me and said in surprise: "Hasan, Hasan! Who do you think I have been with up until this time? Have you seen any fault in my (relationship with) Almighty Allah?

Feeling ashamed at these words I said:

"(Allah Forbid) my Sultan! I meant no such thing. I just dared, as a mere precaution, to suggest that this time that you find yourself might be different from other times" I said.

The great Sultan, having delved into a completely different realm, addressed me for the last time and said:

"Hasan! Read chapter *Yasin*".

With teary eyes, I began to recite. When I came to the verse "Salam (Peace)" the Sultan gave up his honoured spirit to his Lord.

Overall, those who are not with Allah throughout their lives are not subject to this type of favour at their last breath. This is why it is necessary to live our lives with purpose in order to have a fine death.

✿

Sultan Murad II was one who thought not of his own comfort but of gaining the pleasure of Allah. He had a strong will and was very determined to the extent that he did not refrain from sacrificing his life to this end. His biggest concern was to be able to breathe his last breath having faith in his heart and to be able to appear before the presence of Allah on the Day of Gathering blameless and free of sin. After he had married off his son and daughter he said to his vizier, Candarli Ibrahim Pasha:

"O Candarli! Praise be to Allah that we have, with His permission, carried out our duties towards our children in this world. What is now left for us to do is to migrate from here with faith in our hearts...."

✿

Officer Muzaffer, who had displayed great success in the Battle for the Dardanelles, later went to the eastern front where he fought with great courage. Whilst fighting a bloody battle here he was severely wounded. During his last moments when neither his voice nor his eyes could speak, he took out an envelope from his pocket. Then, taking a stick from the ground, he dipped it in the blood that flowed from his wound and began to write:

"Which way is the Qibla (the direction of Mecca)?

Realising that he was about to pass away, those around him immediately granted his request and turned him toward the *Qibla*. At the point of his death, as a last manoeuvre, the Officer turned to give his heroic soldiers the following message. On the one hand, the joy of reunion was written all over his face and yet on the other, there was disquiet and apprehension at the sacred duty he had been given of defending his country:

"Let the squadron continue in its *jihad* for Allah; Do not let my death be in vain…"

He was about to write his third message but he ran out of time. He became a martyr for the sake of his Lord.

What great sensitivity that made him draw blood from his veins when his tongue could no longer speak, in order to explain his need to submit his spirit to his Lord while facing the direction of Mecca. And so the last moments of a life spent in the way of Allah are also blessed and holy.

✿

The state of one of the friends of Allah, Mahmud Sami Ramazanoglu, in his last moments is another good example for us. Sami Efendi was a friend of Allah whose heart was full of love for the Prophet. Just as someone who walks through the snow leaves

241

footprints in the snow; and then one who tries to find their way follows those footsteps. This is how Sami Efendi lived his life, faithfully following in the footsteps of the Prophet. As a display of this he was blessed with passing away in the environs of the Prophet, whom he had spent his entire life following with love and enthusiasm. The moment of his death was the moment that the call to prayer was recited for the *tahajjud* prayer (late night prayer). Those who were with him in those final moments heard only the following words from his lips:

"Allah, Allah, Allah!"...

It was not just his tongue, but his entire body, together with all of its cells and his soul that continually cried out "Allah"...

❀

In short, in order for the slave to depart this life with a beautiful ending, that is to breathe his last breath with faith in his heart, he must first purify his soul and cleanse his heart. He must rid it of its ugly inclinations, and allow it to arrive at a state of being adorned with elevated characteristics, and a place of manifestation of the beautiful names of Almighty Allah. For the heart to reach this state of piety is the most precious gift of guidance in this journey of life. The following lines by Jalaluddin al Rumi explain the nature of purification of the heart:

"You do not make your grave with stones or wood or felt. You must dig your own grave, within your own untainted heart and within the inner purity of your world, in order that you destroy your own claims and self in the face of the exalted Being of Allah".

Then it is necessary to prepare for an eternal realm in the best possible way, with a soul that has been purified, with worship, obedience, and by performing good deeds and giving out.

At the last breath of the slave, Almighty Allah gives him the following good tidings if he is a slave who has embellished his life with good deeds and who has never forgotten his Lord throughout his life:

'The angels descend on those who say, "Our Lord is Allah," and then go straight: "Do not fear and do not grieve but rejoice in the Garden you have been promised' (Fussilat 41:30)

May our Lord bless us all by making us recipients of these glad tidings. Amen!...